Manhood
from the Hood

For Sherry

Manhood
from the Hood

HOW MY GRANDFATHER'S VALUES
INSPIRE MY WORK
WITH AMERICA'S YOUNG MEN

BILL RODDY

Enjoy!

R

BEAVER'S
POND
PRESS

ISBN 10: 1-59298-366-9
ISBN 13: 978-1-59298-366-7

Library of Congress Catalog Number: 2010940833

Printed in the United States of America

First Printing: 2011
Second Printing: 2012

15   14   13   12   5   4   3   2

Cover and interior design by James Monroe Design, LLC.

Beaver's Pond Press, Inc.
7108 Ohms Lane
Edina, MN 55439–2129
(952) 829-8818
www.BeaversPondPress.com

To order, visit www.BeaversPondBooks.com
or call (800) 901-3480. Reseller discounts available.

To my loving grandparents,
William Henry & Minnie C. Roddy,
may you continue to be proud of the man I've become.

Contents

Foreword vii

Prologue ix

Chapter 1 1

Chapter 2 15

Chapter 3 35

Chapter 4 45

Chapter 5 53

Chapter 6 65

Chapter 7 67

Chapter 8 . . . . *75*

Chapter 9 . . . . *77*

Chapter 10 . . . . *85*

Chapter 11 . . . . *87*

Chapter 12 . . . . *91*

Chapter 13 . . . . *95*

Chapter 14 . . . . *101*

Chapter 15 . . . . *109*

Chapter 16 . . . . *113*

Chapter 17 . . . . *117*

Epilogue *123*

Acknowledgements *129*

Foreword

Bill Roddy is a gentle kind of guy. I met him for the first time in the mid-1970s, when he was a college student where I, a priest in my mid-30s, was teaching theology.

Born in Arkansas and raised in Chicago by his hard-working grandparents, Bill had been an outstanding high school basketball player at Chicago's Crane Tech and received scholarship offers from several colleges. Instead, he felt the College of St. Thomas, my alma mater—a small Minnesota school offering only need-based, academic scholarships—was a better fit for him. Indeed, it was. He worked hard in the classroom, while the Tommies' basketball team benefited, too. Bill would score more than 1,400 points in his four years (1975–1979), playing for St. Thomas' legendary coach, Tom Feely. Bill also was chosen to join the President's Student Development Council, a select group of student leaders on campus, as well as the Tiger Club, a select group of student athletes and the guardians of school spirit.

He played tennis, too. So when Bill asked me to play one evening in the summer of 1977, I thought it'd be a friendly, relaxing game between a student and his prof. I liked to think I was a pretty good tennis player, and this affable young guy said he'd just learned the game the summer before. What I didn't know: He had begun to play at Coach Feely's urging. Feely didn't like to lose and almost never did. I should have remembered that. And, what I found out on the court? Neither did Bill. He "schooled me" in humility that day.

Not until the St. Thomas Alumni Association awarded Bill its 2006 Humanitarian Award did I recall the evening of that lesson. Today, as president of what's now the University of St. Thomas, one of the largest Catholic universities in the country, I think of the many teachers who have reinforced it for me.

Humility, along with integrity, industriousness, loyalty, and patience, were the virtues Bill learned from his grandparents, aunts, coaches, and teachers. He remembered them when, as multicultural tennis director for the U.S. Tennis Association, he knew he'd found his life's purpose: to encourage those values by teaching them to young people. So he and his wife, Gail, launched a nonprofit venture, Osiris Organization, to provide at-risk youth with technology and computer training, plus what's really important: meaningful mentorship opportunities that change lives. *Manhood From the Hood* is the story of Bill's inspiring journey toward that goal.

Bill eloquently reminds us that young people—particularly those living in economic, familial, or emotional poverty—need us more than ever before. He has witnessed firsthand, he writes, "the neglect of family values that has caused so much unnecessary pain ... This neglect puts an enormous burden on our communities and our nation." But don't read defeat between those lines. Bill doesn't like losing, and within these pages, he's sketched out a winning game plan.

—Reverend Dennis Dease
President, University of St. Thomas

Prologue

"**H**ey, Mr. Roddy! Man, how'd you learn to play ball like that? And how can you still play ball? Ain't you an old man?"

Playing basketball with the young men at the Hennepin County Home School, a residential adolescent treatment facility in Minnetonka, Minnesota, catapulted me into my life's work and purpose. Young people can be very persistent when they want something.

While I was at the school to teach these adjudicated young men tennis, they would beg me to also get out on the basketball court, but I declined most of the time. My job as multicultural tennis director for the U.S. Tennis Association was to expose more youth of color to the sport of tennis. That's how I ended up at the facility and on the basketball court with them that day. My work in the tennis industry also included several years as a professional tennis instructor. I'd had no intentions of ever playing basketball again. I thought that chapter of my life was completed and closed. I felt happy about the choices I'd made.

When I'd left Chicago in 1975 for a Minnesota college, I had no idea what my life's purpose would be. Later, like many baby boomers who have graduated from college, I worked in the corporate world. But I never felt fulfilled. During those corporate work years, I felt something was missing in my life. When I entered the tennis industry in 1991 and began to have direct contact with young people and their families, I felt instantly fulfilled, because I was helping even in some small way to guide young men and to encourage young women the way so many people had guided and encouraged me.

After we'd finished playing basketball, a lanky, energetic 17-year-old sprinted across the court toward me.

"Hey, Mr. Roddy, do you think you could come and visit me in the cottage this Saturday during family visitation?"

"Will your parents be there as well?"

"No, my mother won't come; I have several younger brothers and sisters at home."

"What about your father?"

"Never met him, Mr. Roddy."

I'd asked him those questions because family visitation day was stressful enough for the young men and their families. I never wanted their parents to feel I had any intent to try to take their parental place. I was a mentor—a support—not a replacement.

1996. It seems like yesterday. I was helping the physical education teacher, Mrs. Leigh Skoglund, implement the tennis program at the Hennepin County Home School when the phone rang.

Mrs. Skoglund motioned me over. "Mr. Roddy, that was the

school principal, Mary Slinde. She would like to talk with you in her office."

"OK, I will head up to her office to see what she wants."

I left the gym and headed to Principal Slinde's office. What could she need from me?

Ms. Slinde was wrapping up a meeting with another teacher. She saw me arrive and waved. She was smiling.

Hmmm. What's this?

"Hi, Mr. Roddy, come in and have a seat. How are you doing today?"

"I am doing OK, Ms. Slinde."

"You are probably wondering why I asked to see you this morning."

"Yes, I am."

"Well, every Monday for the last several months you have dedicated a lot of your time to the young men in the gym with your tennis program, in their cottages, and in their classes. I just wanted to let you know that I have overheard many of the young men walking through the hallways talking about you. They look forward to seeing you on Mondays. They all are in a good mood on Mondays because of you. I just wanted to say thanks."

"Thanks, Ms. Slinde. I had no idea they were enjoying tennis that much."

"Oh no, Mr. Roddy, it's not the tennis. They enjoy *you*. They enjoy being with *you*! You are a wonderful role model for these young men. That's it. I know you want to go back to the gym to be with the students, so I won't hold you up."

Walking back to the gym, I felt a strange sensation come over me. At that moment, I knew what I had to do. My life's purpose was calling.

Chapter

1

Recently, my friend Bernie Aldrich asked me to speak to a group of successful business people on the origins of the nonprofit I co-founded, the Osiris Organization. Bernie and I met in 2006 through mutual friends from the University of St. Thomas in St. Paul, Minnesota. Oddly enough, memories from my early life, mainly about my grandfather, set into motion the introspection that inspired my speech.

After my presentation, many of the business people had more questions about my topic—the values my grandparents had instilled in me. One attendee, Jim Hartfiel, invited me to speak to his Rotary Club because he was so moved by my account of my grandfather's values. At the Rotary Club presentation, I met Greg Rye, who was equally inspired. He encouraged me to speak more about my grandfather's influence in my life and to consider writing a book about it.

Reflections are best shared through life stories. The presentations I had been making opened a flood of emotions. These memories are so much a part of who I am, illustrating why I feel called to do what I do: mentoring America's youth, especially young men.

Marvell, Arkansas, 1957. My mother, Irene, was a teenager when I was born. Our extended family consisted of my grandfather, William Henry Roddy; my grandmother, Minnie Roddy; four aunts, Betty, Samella, Rosella, and Ida, and many cousins in this farming community. After Mom graduated from high school and got married, she moved to Grand Rapids, Michigan. I remained with my grandparents and aunts in Arkansas. I have vivid memories of livestock, fruit trees, gardens and acres of open land, of hunting, fishing and the camaraderie of the men, of huge barbecues with all the attendant sights and smells—of family, community, life.

How hard they all worked on their land! Grandfather was a proud man who valued self-reliance. The only assistance he trusted came from family. My aunts would arrive home from school and quickly dress to work in the fields. Evening brought communion in the form of a family dinner.

In 1962, Grandfather decided to move our family to Chicago. No one knows why. It wasn't up for debate. He decided. Perhaps he thought making more money in the big city would give us a better life.

I was his only son (although I was his grandson, he thought of me as a son). Did he wish to see his daughters unburdened by the challenges of farm maintenance?

In later years, my aunts often told stories of how happy our family was living on our own land, and those stories made a deep impression on me. Our farm was our family business. There was no

30-year mortgage, no credit cards, no concerns about FICA scores or the real estate market. No retirement plans, no stock market investments, no woes about the economy. We were born, lived, died, and respected the rhythm of the land. On the farm, we had learned the benefits of hard work and family values—sharing and self-reliance. We packed those values with our belongings when we journeyed to a new life in Chicago in 1962. Then this strange, foreign, big-city life began to unfold.

After Grandfather found work in a Chicago paper factory and rented a small apartment on the West Side, he sent for my grandmother, my aunts Betty and Ida, and me.

Houses and apartment buildings jammed together. Constant street noise from traffic and the conversations of thousands of people. No chirping birds and insects to awaken us in the mornings as they had down on our farm.

Aunt Betty and I cried, "Daddy, can we go back home to Arkansas? We don't like Chicago!"

But we adjusted. We had no choice. Grandfather was the law, and the law said this was now home. But in those months of transition, we often wept with homesickness.

Aunts Betty and Ida enrolled in high school, headed for graduation. That fall Grandmother enrolled me in kindergarten.

Being left all day with strangers is traumatic for a young child even under the best of circumstances. Imagine going to school for the first time in your life right after a move to a huge, scary city. Chicago in the 1950s and the '60s was filled with African-American families that had migrated from the South to seek jobs in the steel mills and on auto assembly lines. I reflect now on all the children who cried with me that first day of school. Some were nearly hysterical. How many of them had also recently been uprooted from rural life and plunged into big-city chaos? How many were like me, terrified that the happy, secure part of our childhoods had ended, doubting our parents' assurances that the big city offered a better life?

But something good happened to me in that kindergarten class. I met Ernest Leaks there. We share a bond to this day.

In the ensuing years, Ernest and I organized all of our community's Little League baseball and basketball games. He arranged for us to play teams from other communities, and I helped recruit some of the local players. In our neighborhood, baseball was king, so we always had a surplus of guys waiting to play. Most of the games were on Saturday afternoons, and most of the community and family members came to watch us play. There were no coaches; Ernest, the captain, set the lineup and batting order. There was no AAU (Amateur Athletic Union), no coaches, no overbearing parents screaming at the umpires or the players. We just enjoyed the game because we loved it. I played shortstop and left field, and pitched.

After our games, Daddy, which is what I always called my grandfather, would teach me life lessons using sports references. One weekend I hit a grand slam home run. I remember the look on his face. "Son, you guys played well today," he said.

Not "you," but "you guys." My grandfather knew baseball was a team sport. He never wanted me to focus too much on myself.

He'd wear his favorite cap (herringbone; the band was frayed from sweat and wear) when working around our house and attending his beloved White Sox games or watching them on television. During those games, his colorful, nonstop commentary always grabbed my undivided attention.

I knew he was very proud of all of us, but the real lessons came when he took me to see the White Sox play at Comiskey Park. He'd drive down State Street or the Dan Ryan Expressway, exiting off of 35th Street to the ballpark.

We'd pass the Robert Taylor Homes, a public housing project on Chicago's South Side.

"Son, you see all of those buildings over there?"

"Yeah."

"Son, that is no way for people to live. If I have to get four jobs to support our family, then that's what I'll do. We never want the government or anybody else taking care of us. You all are my responsibility, and I will take care of you."

I was learning what "self-reliant" meant. My grandfather was a proud man who valued taking care of his family. For his generation, that was the definition of manhood. I now know that speeches like this were one of his ways of teaching me, his only son, to be responsible and independent.

When I was older, he explained to me that he thought it was OK to use public assistance during a period of transition in one's life. I never heard him judge those who lived in public housing. In that era many hard-working folks, especially those migrating to Chicago from the South, moved into public housing, joining relatives who had migrated earlier. Then they acquired steady employment, saved their money, and transitioned into other housing. My grandfather later explained that he was just afraid that if made a permanent lifestyle, public assistance could destroy a family's work ethic.

Popcorn, hot dogs, peanuts, and being with Daddy at the baseball park—every young boy's dream! The sun rose and set on him and our time at Comiskey Park. In that wonderful place, I bonded with him on many levels.

I wish I could have taped our conversations. Daddy watched the games intensely. He knew baseball; for instance, he could pick out the faults in a pitcher's delivery. He knew all the White Sox players' batting idiosyncrasies. He knew when a pitcher was getting tired or "losing his stuff."

Then, suddenly, he'd casually switch the subject of his concentration.

He looked down at me; his eyes pierced mine. "How is your school work coming?"

"It's OK. I've done all my homework for the week."

Truthfully? What I really was thinking was, "How about another hot dog and box of peanuts?"

Daddy waved his finger toward the players on the field. It was clear to me that he was irritated. "Son, so-and-so couldn't hit a fast-ball if you threw it to him underhanded. Why in the world is he in the cleanup position in the batting order?"

I couldn't care less who struck out or even who won the game. I was with Daddy, eating hot dogs and peanuts on a beautiful summer day.

Comiskey Park with Daddy and meeting Ernest Leaks. Chicago slowly was becoming a bit more inviting.

I'm not sure if my grandfather assigned Aunt Ida the task of making sure I completed my homework and did well in school. Ida, his youngest daughter, had a "warrior" type personality, direct yet loving. There was no misunderstanding Aunt Ida. She meant what she said and didn't care if it hurt your feelings.

I knew she took her mentoring seriously. I had to put the work in or there was a price to pay. Ida made sure that when I got home from school, I did all of my homework and read a half-hour every day, regardless of what my homework assignments were, before I was allowed to go out to play with my friends.

Did she give my grandfather a progress report? I don't know, but the thought of facing Aunt Ida was enough to keep me focused and motivated in school. She was like the *Star Trek* Klingons when they conquer an enemy in battle. Take no prisoners! That was Aunt Ida.

While hovering over me many evenings after school, Aunt Ida made this profound statement to me: "Learn to read well; it is the key to getting a good education. If you can read well, there is no stopping how far you can go. Do you think Mama and Daddy [my grandparents] are going to work every day for nothing? They didn't have the chance to succeed that we have today. They were denied the opportunities when they were growing up in the South. They expect more out of us."

All my friends in our inner-city community had family members who truly cared for us. It was common for both parents, and sometimes other relatives as well, to attend open houses at school. My grandfather and grandmother sent Aunt Betty or Aunt Ida to those open houses, and the aunts would report back to my grandparents.

My friends took pride in getting good grades in school. Believe it or not, there was always competition among the boys over who got the most As or Bs on report cards, over who won the spelling quizzes that week. We loved sports, but sports were not the obsession they are today.

Aunt Ida married, divorced, and had several children of her own while living with us—Gwen, Matthew, Andrea, and later Frederick. I felt like I was one of her kids. She made sure that I, my grandparents' first grandchild, didn't demonstrate any behavior that veered from our grandparents' work ethic.

During my high school years, Ida's mentoring and discipline, along with my love of reading, helped me excel. Aunt Ida. She personified tough love.

Those years were an intense, important time in American history. I remember the civil rights movement, hearing Dr. Martin Luther King Jr., the speeches of Malcolm X, the Vietnam War protests. My aunts told me stories about how a brave woman in Alabama, Rosa Parks, stood up for all of us when she refused to give up her seat and move to the back of the bus, and about boxer Muhammad Ali. While warming up for one of our baseball games, Ernest and I talked about Ali's religion-based refusal to fight in the Vietnam War.

For young kids, that was quite a deep conversation. But we were well aware of the social movements of the era. It was a time of struggle for equal opportunities and equal education. We knew the sacrifices our parents were making, and we could see those sacrifices coming to fruition in the civil rights movement. Their struggle consumed us all.

Meanwhile, Aunt Ida and I bumped heads daily. I'd ask myself, "Why is she so hard on me? Why should I have to do all this hard work when my friends are at the playground playing baseball and tag?"

During the 1960s, our elders talked constantly about learning to read well and making good use of our ability to acquire an education because many of them had been denied that right. They worked unceasingly to make sure that we were not denied this important attribute.

And so, much love to Aunt Ida and her persistence about reading. I often wonder what direction my life would have taken without her in my life during those years.

Aunt Betty, Ida's older sister, was the ultimate counselor to me. She too married, divorced, and was raising her own son, Juan, and her daughter, Minnie Yvonne. Tareef, Lenard, and Laki came later. Aunt Betty treated me like one of her own. In a loving voice, she would explain everything Aunt Ida was doing, but in a way that made more sense to me. Despite their different styles, Betty and Ida had great respect for each other. I only saw them argue once.

Betty helped me to understand that Daddy and Mama, my grandparents, wanted a better life for us. She told me about the conditions they'd faced in the segregated South, because I was too young to understand the deep-rooted discrimination pervasive in that time and culture and how it had affected my own family.

One day, Betty told me, Daddy had taken some of our crops into downtown Marvell, Arkansas, thinking he would get a fair price. He came home disappointed with the prices he received from the white Southern wholesalers. I think this is why he taught us to never trust anyone outside of our family.

How Aunt Betty knew all of this amazed me. At times I felt like it was information overload, too much for a young kid to handle. I'd listen, but usually I just wanted to go out and play baseball with my friends.

But I did often wonder what it would have felt like to work for thirteen hours a day on a farm, to take your produce to market for sale and be denied a fair price. How long could you do that without your pride taking a beating? Aunt Betty said it was not so much about the money. After all, our farm provided everything we needed. But for Daddy, it was the sense of pride he felt working the fields, producing the crops, and reaping the harvest.

How did Daddy handle the disrespect, hearing the fair price the wholesalers gave to the white farmers who brought *their* crops to market? "Take pride in the work you do. Never hate anyone," Daddy told us all the time.

Aunt Betty had a wonderful way of making sense out of everything in my life. I don't know if she knows how her wisdom influenced my young mind.

Oh, she was preparing me for much more to come.

Twin aunts Samella Smith and Rosella Smith (each married unrelated men with the Smith surname) had already moved to Chicago in 1959 and 1961, respectively. Trained as nurses, they found better employment opportunities in the city.

Aunt Sam is an angel, the definition of unconditional love. She offered lots of hugs during the times when I needed them the most. Most of them came after run-ins with Aunt Ida over homework assignments she claimed I had missed.

Aunt Sam married and had three sons, Wayne, Demetrius, and Timothy. Her sons felt more like brothers to me than cousins; such was the bond we had as a family. Aunt Sam had her own apartment and was always gainfully employed.

Nursing fit Aunt Sam perfectly. She'd tell me stories about her patients bonding with her and feeling sad about leaving the hospital even though they were going home to their own families. Sam was always the first to unconditionally help a family member or relative; she was our Mother Teresa.

She told me many stories of how at ages two and three I'd followed her and the rest of my aunts around the farm. It had been difficult for me to pronounce her first name, so I had called her "Yam," she said.

As I'd tagged along with them, my three-year-old legs would fall behind. Afraid, I'd call out to her, "Don't leave me, Yam!" She'd stop whatever she was doing, come back, pick me up, and carry me back to our house.

Every time she tells me that story, it brings tears to my eyes. I feel fortunate to have had someone love me that much.

As an adolescent growing up in Chicago, I always looked forward to spending weekends at Sam's apartment. I knew when I needed to be with her, and she always obliged. It was not what she said to me. It was how she made me feel as a person. With her, I always felt the world was a safe place.

Aunt Rosella (Ro) arrived in Chicago in 1959. She too was trained as a nurse. Aunt Ro was very independent. She eventually married and had kids of her own, Tony, Kenny, Sandra, Stephanie, and Nicholas.

I did not spend as much time with Aunt Ro as I did with my other aunts. She lived on the South Side and was busy working and taking care of her family.

Still, many times my grandfather and I took trips to her house on the South Side to make sure she was OK. I remember Grandfather taking me along a few times to help her move into increasingly better housing. In her last move, she purchased a home on the South Side in which she still lives today.

One morning Ro called us to say that someone had thrown paint all over the front of her house. Her neighborhood had begun to integrate, and apparently some of the locals did not want a young African-American family living among them. Within a few years, more black families moved in seeking the American dream, and the former residents fled.

In my household, we did not preach hate. So it was baffling to my young self that people felt and acted with such hatred and cruelty. I was naïve. Chicago had a way of waking you up to the real world.

Aunt Ro worked hard and sent all of her kids to private Catholic schools in Chicago. All my aunts lived their parents' values, prizing education, reading, independence, and self-reliance.

Grandmothers take great pleasure in every moment with their grandchildren. I have never known a grandparent who could look a grandchild in the eye and say "no."

"Grandma, could you take us hang-gliding off Mount Kiliman-jaro next week?"

"OK, honey, let me take a few pain pills to make sure my back holds up. Now, Grandma can only do this once, OK, honey?"

"Grandma, are we going to have some milk and cookies, too?"

"Yes, honey, you know Grandma can't have you going hungry."

"Thanks, Grandma! We like coming to visit you!"

Imagine living full time with your grandmother, who loves you every moment. This was my childhood.

Grandmother was born in 1919 in rural Arkansas. She married my grandfather when she was just fifteen. Traditional Southern values shaped Grandmother. If a guest arrived at our house, he or she was always invited to eat. If it were Sunday morning, you'd find her at church.

Grandmother's most memorable statement to me was, "Son, always treat people the way you want to be treated." As I reflect on this, it reminds me of Mahatma Gandhi's statement "Be the change in the world that you want to see."

She would teach me these things as I sat in the kitchen as she stirred her pots. I'd wait to eat the cake batter left in the bowl. "Mama, can I have the rest of the cake mix?" She never said no.

I did not have a lot of clothes, but Grandmother always made sure that those I had were clean. It seems to me that in those days, working-class folks were like that. They took pride in caring for what they had even though they didn't have a lot. I don't remember any keeping-up-with-the-Joneses attitude.

Grandmother would say, "Son, always remember acts of kindness." Then I would go out and see a fight in our neighborhood over something insignificant, or acts of total cruelty. To my young mind, this was so disturbing and confusing. This consternation followed me through my high school years as well.

To protect myself emotionally, I unconsciously sought out friends who seemed to have similar family values.

Birth is a humbling, awesome experience to witness. A precious gift.

Irene was my grandparents' oldest daughter. After giving birth to me in 1957, she married, moved to Michigan, and had six more children.

I am here living and breathing because of my mother, Irene. Growing up, I did not live with her, but during summer vacations

I'd visit her and my siblings in Michigan.

The reasons why I had stayed with my grandparents rather than moving to Michigan to live with Irene didn't weigh on my mind. So many family members in Chicago showered me with love. Long ago I had accepted that my aunts and grandparents cared for me very well.

As a baby, I had sandy brown hair, so "Sandy" is my nickname among family in Michigan. To this day, I feel love and affection when I am called Sandy; it brings a big, warm smile to my face.

Irene was the first person in our family to earn a degree from a university. She worked in the Michigan school system. Her husband, Osbe Hoskins Sr., worked in the construction industry. My mother and I have a loving relationship to this day.

My six siblings, Calvert, Joanne, Osbe Jr., Myron, Rose, and Carolyn, were great students and formidable athletes in high school and college. Osbe Jr. and I think that all of the athletic talent in our family came from our grandfather and Irene, but we had to work at developing it. My siblings were outstanding in the classroom as well as in the field. They are in high school and college halls of fame.

Cal, Osbe Jr., and Myron are wonderful fathers to their children. I always try to call them on Father's Day to express how proud I am of them as fathers. Great fathering is a family tradition.

I wasn't as close to my sisters, Joanne, Rose, and Carolyn, when we were growing up. But now that we have gotten older, we all are much closer, and I enjoy talking with them.

Even though I was not raised with my brothers and sisters, I have a very deep connection with all of them, and they know I love them. Much love to the wonderful lady who gave me life, Irene Hoskins.

Chapter 2

I was very involved in sports. I loved baseball and attending White Sox games with my grandfather. Our community Little League baseball team played an important role in reinforcing my family's values. The most important thing Little League did was to help me develop a lifelong relationship with Ernest Leaks. We remain great friends to this day.

What I admire most about Ernest is his loyalty to his family and friends. When you became his friend, he was always there for you. He was a great judge of a person's character, and I believe this is because of his family's value system. I admired how he respected his mother and stepfather. Our generation learned to respect our elders, both within our family and outside of it.

Ernest's older brothers had many friends in the community, and no one messed with them. They were the "Klingons" of our community. Ernest was able to handle himself in any situation, but if he needed help, he would call the Klingons, who quickly got everyone back on track. They were judge, jury, and community corrections officers!

Ernest and I attended the same elementary school, middle school, and Crane High School. He was outstanding in math, and could have been a mathematician. I read a lot, so I was good at spelling. We helped each other with class work without being asked.

We bonded through sports and in the classroom. We gravitated to basketball. Maybe we just got tired of all of the organizing it took for the baseball games against other communities; it did not take young minds long to want to do something different. We did not abandon baseball when we embraced basketball, but we played less organized baseball.

We fell in love with basketball in gym class. Our gym teacher, Mr. Gladstone Trotter, played with us and taught us the rules. He scheduled little tournaments for us during our gym period. That was it; we were hooked on the game. To this day, I know I gravitated to basketball because I wanted to be with Ernest and learn and grow with him.

Many older youths helped us develop our basketball skills. We'd stand on the sidelines of the playground and watch them play. One was a guy we called "Fink." (In Chicago, we all had nicknames.) Fink took a liking to Ernest and me. I lived only three blocks from Fink, so I saw him often.

One day I was in the local community store and Fink was there with friends shooting pool. We started talking, and Fink said that I needed a nickname. He said I looked like a cartoon character called Ignatz, pronounced "Ick-nag," in George Herriman's cartoon series *Krazy Kat*. This cartoon concept originated in a comic strip in the 1930s and in the 1960s was presented as a cartoon. Why Fink decided to name me this was a moment in time we will never under-stand. In those days, you never chose your own nickname. Someone respected had to give it to you. Once you got one, everyone in the community honored it and called you by it. It was a crazy way of showing respect and affection.

After that, all of my friends in Chicago called me Nag. The character was a mischievous mouse who always threw bricks at people. The female character Krazy Kat was in love with Ignatz. Fink said I had the same eyes as the mouse. To this day, Ernest will always be Brother Ern to me, and I'm forever Nag to him.

Fink was influential in our community, but had personal challenges and demons. When we started playing in basketball tour-naments, it was Fink who coached and encouraged us. He taught us about many aspects of basketball, and he also taught us to stay away from drugs and alcohol. Here's a paradox: We all knew he used drugs, but we also knew that he was sincere, that he didn't want us to do anything that would harm our abilities. He saw basketball as a vehicle for us to move forward with our lives.

I know many may find this hard to believe, but in those days even the drug users encouraged us to stay in school, to stay out of trouble, and to avoid drugs or alcohol.

Ernest and I never judged the dealers and users. They were still our role models outside of our family. For one thing, they were all great basketball players. We wanted to learn the game and to become better players, so we did not judge those who excelled in it. We never saw them use drugs in our presence, but we remembered their words of encouragement. They seemed to have accepted their fates and for some reason didn't see any alternatives in their own lives. But they wanted more for us. After the games ended, they hung around, talked about their lives and the mistakes they'd made. I'd listen to every word.

Another Fink in the community was a guy we called Ing. He was bright and insightful about what was happening in our country during that time.

There were many other such influential figures in our community, and regardless of their personal situations, they really cared about the young people. They believed in the concept that it takes a village to raise a child. If we got out of line, they were the first ones to discipline us verbally.

Not all the Finks used or dealt drugs. Most were hard-working family men who had blue-collar jobs. Some attended local high schools. On the weekends, they all played basketball in our community. We hung on the sidelines, watching their every move.

Fink told us we had to start watching some real "ballers" and encouraged us to start going to the Gladstone Middle School playground. Gladstone was attached to a city recreational facility and had organized leagues. Some of the best athletes in the city played there in the summer. Most of the local legends lived blocks from the school.

I'll never forget Fink. A couple of years ago, Ernest called with the terrible news that someone had robbed Fink and then shot him dead because he apparently didn't give them the money fast enough.

Ernest went into great detail of how Fink had turned his life around. He had stopped using drugs and alcohol and had become a drug and alcohol counselor at a social service agency. Listening to Ernest talk about Fink that evening made me so proud to have had a person like Fink in my life while I was young. Even when he used drugs and alcohol, Fink had values that Ernest and I admired. They were the same values our families held. Fink was in our lives for reasons unknown to us at the time. He was the perfect example of how anyone with the desire to change the direction of his or her life can do so.

That night, after my long talk with Ernest about Fink and his influence on our young minds, I cried.

We embraced Fink's recommendation to watch the other neighborhood players, a.k.a. the "ballers." Ballers are basketball players who develop their skills to the point where they stand out among their peers. They set the standards to which we all aspired.

The ballers lived on the east side of Damen Street. When you crossed Damen Street, basketball took on a whole new meaning. We all felt it. We young men were in awe!

Ernest was good at getting to know all of the important contacts across Damen. He arranged for us to play in tournaments during the summer.

I remember the first couple of days we ventured across Damen Street to see the ballers. Ernest knew those who were playing in high school and the up-and-coming ones transitioning to high school.

One weekend, Ernest, myself, and several other young fans arrived at Gladstone Middle School to watch an organized basketball game. Entering the playground area, we could feel the aura of greatness; we were easily inspired. People gathered around the court watching the ballers' every move.

I couldn't believe what I witnessed! "Ernest, who is that dude who just hit those last two jump shots?"

"Oh, that's Fat, he's Heavy's younger brother."

"Who is Heavy?"

"Melvin 'Heavy' Freeman is one of the refs and a freshman who plays ball at Crane High. Crane is where all the ballers in our community play. Nag, the whole Freeman family is full of ballers."

After the game, Ernest approached Verneil "Fat" Freeman and talked to him about his performance. Ernest was not the shy type when it came to introducing himself to people he wanted to know. I stood right by his side listening to him interview Fat about basketball. Fat talked about the skills he had learned from his older brothers, Heavy and Little Hook. He talked about the hours of practice and dedication it had taken to develop his skills.

After that conversation, Ernest and I felt even more inspired. We knew what we had to do. We had to put the time in, which meant practice, practice, and more practice if we wanted to achieve Fat's skill level. Fat verified what Fink told us about putting the time in—that there were no shortcuts to becoming a good baller.

We walked back across Damen Street to our side of the community. Ernest talked about Fats' brothers, Heavy and Jerome "Little Hook" Freeman, and their basketball skills. Heavy, a playground legend, was a freshman player at Crane High. Ernest went on and on about Heavy's abilities and about Little Hook. There was a middle brother, Michael "Ice Man" Freeman, and an older brother, George "Big Hook" Freeman. Ernest said Little Hook was the greatest baller to ever come out of Crane. He relayed stories from Gladstone Middle School locals about some of the moves Little Hook used on the playground and at Crane High.

I loved playing basketball, and at the same time I was starting to understand some of my grandfather's values. His values and Ernest's were compatible. One in particular was working hard on something you valued.

But those values also created conflict within me and began to weigh on my consciousness. I struggled now. It was a heavy load for a kid to try to carry.

How could I focus on understanding and living my grandfather's value system and at the same time dedicate so much time and energy to my newfound love of basketball? These conflicts burdened me. I was really trying to make sense of life.

You might think that a young man of that age would be incapable of such introspection. But in the 1960s, thinking about larger social issues and how they affected our individual lives was common for young and old alike.

My grandfather had his own opinions. Frequently he'd express to me that as a community we had to be careful about asking outsiders to help us, or to give us this or that.

"Son, we need to come together and build our own schools if that is what is needed," he'd say; passion—maybe even a little anger—welling up in his voice. "Don't let me *ever* hear or see you asking someone to do something for you that you can do yourself!"

Daddy was a robust man. His hands bore rough calluses from many hard-laboring years on the farm in Arkansas and in the paper factory in Chicago. He stood about 5 feet 10, with a dark complexion and a deep, masculine voice. His verbal delivery, while few in words, and his demeanor were alert, interested, and parental.

Many weekends when he would work under his 1965 Ford Galaxy 500, I'd watch him.

"Son, come over here," he'd say. "I want to show you how to change the brake pads and tune up a car."

"OK." I peered under the car.

"This is how I put the new pads on…. Now, come over here and let me show you how to put the next one on."

My little hands would follow his directions and he would watch with excitement.

"There you go, son; that's how you do it," he'd say with pride.

Once we'd finish I'd want to go play with my friends. We all had miniature racing cars. Sometimes several of my friends and I would take the bus to a hobby shop that had a custom racing track. Once after I had helped my grandfather with his car, I asked for two dollars for bus fare and fees for the hobby shop.

"Daddy, do you have two dollars? I want to race my cars with my friends," I'd ask.

"OK," my grandfather would say. "You did a good job helping me, and you earned the two dollars."

He continued: "I only want you to accept money from others that you have earned," he admonished. "Never accept anything from anyone that you don't earn. Do you understand me?"

"Yeah," I responded. I'd heard him, but at the time I did not fully understand. All I was thinking about was the two dollars I was getting so that I could go race my cars with friends. Little did I know this would be one of many teaching moments about his values that would stay in my mind.

That era raised our consciousness. We all dealt with it in different ways. Mine was an introspective approach, as I tried to live a value system taught by loved ones, to establish friends outside of my family and to piece it all together. I kept my thoughts and feelings private until I was older and able to make sense of them.

My grandfather's strict values, independence, and self-reliance, and his emphasis on education and reading, had a powerful effect on me. He even forbade me to eat at someone else's house because he believed strongly that only he should provide me with food and shelter.

There were so many questions I kept secret but pondered incessantly:

Why are we so cruel to one another?

Why is there so much racial hatred in Chicago?

Is the rest of the world like Chicago?

Why don't white people live in our neighborhood?

Why do men treat women the way they do?

Why is Aunt Ida making me read so much?

I started to realize it would take total dedication to obtain the basketball skills of our local legends.

Would I ever be as good a basketball player as Fat and Heavy were?

Did I really want to dedicate so much time and energy to basketball? To what end?

Would my lack of dedication affect my relationship with Ernest and Fink? Could I live with that?

Sometimes when I played basketball, my mind would focus on trying to understand my surroundings and not disappointing my basketball friends. These friends made it clear that they believed I was talented. Fink's expectations were high; he lived and breathed basketball. Would I be able to balance all of these expectations? I didn't want to disappoint anyone.

I eventually failed to live up to my friends' basketball expectations—especially Fink's. My confidence started to suffer. I lacked the confidence to excel because I could not bring myself to dedicate all of my energy to basketball. As a result, I endured many demeaning comments from friends, acquaintances, and even coaches (many of them too vulgar to share here) during those middle school and high school years. During those sometimes painful and confusing school years, I never shared these experiences with anyone. Not family. Not friends.

Throughout that time, Ernest remained supportive and encouraging. Brother Ern's loyalty as a friend helped me tremendously during those times.

As a young man who loved his grandparents and aunts, I obeyed their values without question. But secrets and internal conflict continued to haunt me.

What high school should we attend? Crane was where all of the ballers went, so we followed.

Some of my middle school teachers wanted me to go to more academically challenging high schools. I knew they meant well, but they didn't understand my connection with Ernest.

Round about then, my grandfather purchased our first home farther out west of the city. The area was called K-Town because many of the streets started with a K: Keeler, Kostner, etc. We lived on Jackson Boulevard. In the summer of 1972, we packed up and moved into our new home.

K-Town was an area of Chicago that never felt like home. Constantly on edge, we waited for the next crisis.

I wondered if my grandfather had done any research on the area. Why had he purchased our first home in such an area?

I befriended many youths in our new neighborhood. On the first day at our new house, a youth my age came to our front porch and introduced himself. Romero (I never did learn his last name) lived just two houses down from us.

We made small talk for a while. "Do you like basketball?" Romero asked me. "Yes, I do," I replied. He invited me to shoot hoops with him at a playground a few blocks away. We played one-on-one for a while.

"OK," Romero said. "I've had enough! Where did you learn to play ball like that?"

I told him about Fink, Ernest, and the legends in my former community. But mainly I mentioned the time I had spent practicing and that I would be trying out for the team at Crane High School. Crane's basketball reputation was known throughout Chicago.

"Man, Crane always has great ballers!" Romero said. "Do you think you are going to make the team?"

"I don't know, but I will try out for the JV team this upcoming school year, my freshman year."

Romero was instrumental in introducing me to all of the local basketball players. Some were gang members who liked me right away because of my basketball skills. They all wanted me on their teams during pickup games. The gang leaders admired and respected good ballers. I got to know most of them, but I couldn't live the gang culture. So I had to use basketball as a diplomat might have. I used it as a bridge, as a safety net between the two worlds.

Romero and I were once robbed at gunpoint. We were so scared and mad. We didn't recognize the two young men, but all we would have had to do was find out their names, then report the incident to some of the gang leaders we knew. Restitution would have been resolved by gang rules.

Imagine a high school freshman learning two codes of honor—my grandfather's code and the gang code. Why should a child have to choose? But choose I did. Romero and I let the whole incident go. The amount of money and our bruised egos were not worth someone's life. Besides, the price might have been too high to pay—a possible induction into a gang.

The area was full of gangs and drive-by shootings. During the summer months, there was at least one shooting a week. I felt like I was a soldier (or civilian) in the rice paddies in Vietnam.

Ernest and I made the junior varsity team as freshmen at Crane High School. That same year, Heavy was a senior and one of our local legends. His original position was guard, but he was an intelligent player who understood all of the positions extremely well. He played center that year. What versatility! The team was full of great guards—Nate Williams, Donald Brown, Patrick Hazelwood, and James Jackson. That year the varsity team made it to the Illinois state high school basketball tournament. We called it "going down state" when a public school team from the city made it to the state tournament.

All of the teams that made it down state had to endure extreme competition from other schools in the city and other regions. If your team made it out of its region by playing other city schools, it had to go to the sectionals and then super-sectionals. If your team prevailed, it was battle-tested and ready for the big show down state against the state's best.

Ernest and I didn't get much playing time in during our freshman year while on JV, but we were just happy to be on the team. There were so many other negative activities to tempt young men in K-Town. The pull to join a gang and to sell drugs was strong for so many. It was all around us daily, but basketball and my family were my sanctuaries. They kept me focused.

Aunt Betty was the only family member to watch me play a basketball game during my senior year. I remember the game, on Parents Night. All of the games started at 3:30 p.m. on weekdays. My grandfather and grandmother had regular 8–5 jobs and could not get home until 6 or 6:30 p.m.

Most of our parents worked in such blue-collar jobs and therefore could not attend games. As young people of that era, we knew they had to work, so we did not consider their attendance mandatory.

We would never have been able to imagine our parents informing their supervisor, "My son is playing in a basketball game this evening and I need to leave at 2:30 in order to make his 3:30 game." Surely a pink slip would have awaited that parent the next day! We never thought about asking our parents to take off from work to watch us play. Still, at the Crane High School basketball games, it was standing room only.

During those years, Aunt Betty and I had many conversations. Most of them took place late in the evenings, and most revolved around how I should refrain from getting young girls pregnant. Aunt Betty stressed to me that I didn't need such complications in my life and that I should focus on going to college.

Like my grandmother, Aunt Betty was petite. When she

really wanted to get my attention and understanding, she would lower her voice. At such times, her voice vibrated like smooth jazz on my young ears. In her voice and her countenance, Aunt Betty represented the balancing energy between Aunt Ida's no-nonsense authority and Aunt Sam's unlimited love.

"Little Henry," she'd say (I was named after my grandfather, and the nickname was a reflection of him). "Make something out of yourself by going to college and getting an education. You know this is what Mama and Daddy want for you."

It was her way of saying that there is more to life waiting for you and that you shouldn't delay the realization of your destiny by bringing kids into the world who you were not capable of taking care of with young girls you didn't intend to marry.

I can still see her face as she shared her thoughts and insights about the disappointment my grandparents would feel if I brought a child into the world while I was still a child myself. The shame and disappointment would have been very heavy burdens for a young mind to carry. Aunt Betty broke it down for me, and it made sense.

For some reason, I always knew our conversations were meant for my ears only, and so I never spoke of them to anyone else. I kept them close to my mind and heart and often reflected on them.

My family played out the strong hand, the royal flush of guilt, shame, and fear of disappointing them. The hand was played with love, though. And it worked. What game might I be playing right now without that strong suit played out years ago?

Junior year, I made the varsity team. Ernest got lots of playing time off the bench. This was Albert Brown's first year as varsity coach, and I never played that year. Coach expressed his disappointment in my lack of confidence, many times in a very demeaning way, and he and I really didn't develop much of a relationship. But I stayed on and supported my teammates, and the team remained my sanctuary away from home. James Jackson and Andre "Champ" Wakefield were the team's stars that year.

I do remember a very funny moment from that time. Ernest "E-Thang" Williams introduced me to hard rock music. I also experimented with smoking marijuana (reefer) with him.

"Nag, hard rock sounds better when you got your high on," E-Thang bragged.

After a couple of weeks of getting high with E-Thang, the thrill wore off. But I still listened to the music. While in our locker room after a game, E-Thang played a joke on the team. He brought in a tape player, turned up the volume as loud as it could go, and blasted out "Whole Lotta Love" by Led Zeppelin. All of the other players thought we had lost our minds.

E-Thang and I listened not only to Led Zeppelin but bands like Yes, Jimi Hendrix, Robin Trower, and Black Sabbath. Sacrilege! African-Americans were supposed to listen only to R&B. If our teammates could have had us committed to a psych ward, they would have done so without hesitation. The only way we then could have been released from the psych ward in their view would have been to maybe attend classes and play in the basketball games. After that we would be locked back up!

I recall James Jackson screaming at the top of his lungs, "E-Thang, you and Nag turn off that bullshit music. Don't nobody want to hear that shit! What the fuck is wrong with you two motherfuckers?"

Of course E-Thang and I doubled over with laughter as we left the locker room. Two young African-American guys with huge Afros listening to hard rock played by a bunch of long-haired white guys! Yes, sacrilege.

I spent a lot of time talking to Aunt Betty and helping my grandfather around the house. He was the kind of man who would never ask for help, who would exhaust himself before he would consider asking for any type of assistance.

It was a very tough year for me because I was reflecting so deeply about the many contradictions at play in my life. For one thing, I had come to realize that my grandparents were human just like everyone else.

One day I answered the phone and it was a bill collector. She asked for my grandfather. He happened to be walking past me on his way toward the back of our house.

"May I speak to Mr. Roddy, please?"

"Daddy, some lady on the phone wants to talk to you."

"Who is it?" Daddy looked irritated. Toward me? I wasn't sure.

"May I ask who is calling, please?" She said she was so-and-so from X company.

"Hey Daddy, it's so-and-so from X company." I was hollering out to my grandfather with the lady listening on the other end of the line.

"Tell her I'm not here."

"I'm so sorry, Ms. So-and-So, but my father is not here."

"Tell your father that he needs to take care of his outstanding bill with us," she said ever so politely.

"Daddy, she said it was some kind of bill you owed them."

My grandfather did not say a word, but his piercing look stopped me cold. What did that look mean?

Before we purchased our home in K-Town, I had wondered why we moved a lot on the West Side.

My grandfather had such pride that he could *make* money. But did this incident indicate that he had issues with *managing* money?

Did he get pissed off over owing landlords and say, "Hell with it, I will just move my family"?

Was he embarrassed at not being on top of his finances as the patriarch of our family?

Did that phone call reveal a flaw in him, thus making him perhaps less worthy of my respect?

My grandparents never talked to us about finances. Their generation did not share that type of information with kids. I often wondered how much money we had. I would accompany my grandfather to the bank and he would talk to me about paying bills, but he never shared details. Most of the time we went to get money orders to pay bills, and I remember seeing him put some money into a savings account.

I never wanted for anything, never lacked clothing or food. But we never talked about the money that provided these things. Could poor money management have been the reason money was such a taboo subject?

Aunt Betty asked me to take a more active role in mentoring her kids, Juan, Minnie, Von, Tareef, Laki, and Lenard. Juan, her oldest son, loved to watch me play baseball at our local playground after school. I did the best I could to always be positive and support them.

High school started to feel like a burden. My classes were not that challenging, and I had a study hall in my schedule. Study halls were temporary holding pens as far as I was concerned. Nobody studied in them, so I felt I didn't need to attend them. I started to skip study hall.

About two weeks after I started skipping them, my grandmother met me in the living room and screamed at me about a letter she had received from Crane High saying that I was skipping classes. The letter did not indicate that it was a study hall I had skipped and that I was getting As and Bs in all of my other classes. It just said that I was skipping classes.

That evening she approached me, wearing a flowered apron. She was making biscuits and frying chicken, and had flour all over her hands. Drawing up her full 5 feet 1 stature, she glared up at me. As she shook her finger at me, some of the flour dusted my face. Nothing I could do or say appeased her. I had to listen to her rant and rave for about ten minutes before she cooled down.

She had contacted Aunt Ida, who arrived to see what all of the commotion was about. Aunt Ida, a.k.a. Klingon Warrior, approached me.

"Aunt Ida, please let me explain the letter to you and Mama," I pleaded. "I am not skipping any of my major classes. This is just a study hall the students go to. Nobody does any studying and it's boring. Why should I have to go?"

The two women—grandmother and aunt—stared at me as though I'd lost my mind.

"You need to go to them because they are on your schedule," Aunt Ida said. "Mama and Daddy don't know the difference because the letter did not say what classes you were skipping. Don't miss any more study halls, and I don't ever want to see this type of letter coming here again, or I will make sure Daddy finds out."

That's all she had to say. I never missed another one.

I had violated an important component of our family values—respecting education—and was quickly brought back into line by loved ones. There was no negotiation; I was "guilty" for skipping classes and the jury had made its decision. Obey the family values or there will be hell to pay. Case closed!

Around this time, however, adolescence abruptly pulled aside the veil of childhood innocence covering my eyes. I could no longer deny two huge elephants standing in the living room. We all knew about them but wouldn't openly acknowledge it. I wanted to yell out, "What the hell? Would somebody explain to me how this shit fits into our family values?"

It was clear *I* had to live under my grandparents' strict non-negotiable code of values. But by my senior year, it was also clear to me that my grandparents were human. Or was it worse? Were they human all along, but had their godlike status blinded my child's eyes? I felt very confused about what I now witnessed. My grandparents, I had discovered, engaged in activities that fell short of their values, activities that would have sent *me* straight to judgment and punishment.

When we first moved to Chicago in 1962, my grandmother did not work outside the home. Grandfather was at work. Aunt Ida and Aunt Betty were attending high school. I was in kindergarten. Aunt Ida shared with me that during those early years, my grandmother frequently went next door to our neighbors' house and had a few drinks. She had lots of time on her hands. According to Aunt Ida, it started with a few drinks in those early years and then escalated. By the time I was in high school, my sweet grandmother had serious issues with alcohol. She was belligerent, angry, cursing, disruptive to the entire household. But no one said a word about it. Why not?

I wondered why at times she appeared to be so unhappy but so loving to her grandkids, especially me. When she drank, she would rant, making sure everyone knew (for the umpteenth time) about her disappointment in her childhood and in how she was treated.

Why did she scream at my grandfather some late nights when we lived in K-Town? It made for many sleepless nights. Was it that he ignored her, or was there more to her concerns? It never occurred to me to ask her.

On one occasion, my Aunt Ida and I did try to get my grandmother into treatment, but failed. She did eventually stop drinking.

All I knew and will always know is that I love her. She remains my grandmother, who loved me with all her heart. I would not be the person I am today without her love. She was able to provide me with unconditional love and support despite her own imperfections. She passed away in 2006. May she continue to rest in peace!

My grandfather never showed my grandmother any physical affection. As a child, I guess I didn't really notice, at least not enough to think much of it. But as a young man in college I often wondered, why not? When I would come home to visit from college, I would notice his increasing emotional distance from my grandmother and me.

Why didn't anyone talk about these issues with my grandparents? That's a rhetorical question, because I know why not. In those days, especially in the African-American community, *it just wasn't done.*

These two elephants in the living room—Grandmother's alcohol abuse during my last two years in high school and Grandfather's marital coldness—simply took up residence. We all just tiptoed around them. And as far as I understood at the time, this is what we were supposed to do. Only much later would I discover how seriously my grandfather had strayed from his values.

In her splendid checkered jumper, teacher Ms. Daniels set an example for her well-dressed afternoon kindergarten class at Brainard Elementary School in Chicago, Illinois, in November 1962. Among her neatly dressed, solemn-faced students were Bill Roddy and his good friends Ernest Leaks and Gregory Bingham.

Bill's Aunt Betty, shown here in 2004, was a guiding angel during his formative years in Chicago. Sadly, Betty passed away in 2009.

Bill Roddy and Ernest "Brother Ern" Leaks, a childhood pal
who became a friend for life, in August 2010.

Bill Roddy, right, with
Walter "Junior Man"
Green, a dear friend of
his Chicago youth, in
August 2010.

Despite a hardscrabble existence on the family farm in Arkansas, Bill Roddy, the little boy in the foreground, had reason to smile in this 1960 photo. Aunt Ida, kneeling at left; his grandmother, Minnie C. Roddy; and his grandfather, William Henry Roddy.

A proud college graduate, Bill Roddy posed in May 1979 with two of his Chicago aunts, Samella "Sam" and Ida, after his four years at the College of St. Thomas (now the University of St. Thomas) in St. Paul, Minnesota.

Back row: Uncle Earl Newsome, Aunt Dora Newsome,
Bill's great-grandmother "Big Mamma" Newsome, Aunt Samella Smith,
and Bill's grandmother, Minnie C. Roddy. Front row: Bill Roddy and
his younger half-brothers, Calvert and Myron Hoskins, and his nephew,
Demetrius Smith.

Irene Roddy Hoskins gave
birth to Bill Roddy in
Arkansas 1957 when she was
just a teenager. She went on
to marry Osbe Hoskins Sr.
and to raise six more children
in Michigan while Bill was
being brought up by her
parents in Arkansas and
Chicago. Over the years, Bill
developed a close relationship
with his mother and her other
children. This photo was
taken in 2008.

Coach Willie White, one of Bill's basketball coaches at Crane High School in Chicago, in 1975. Coach White told his players, "Basketball is a chess game in motion." He died in the late 1980s.

The colorfully nicknamed Freeman brothers, a.k.a. "the ballers" from the east side of Damen Street in inner-city Chicago, were a basketball powerhouse in the 1960s and '70s. Here they are in a 2009 photo: bottom row, Jean Freeman, George "Big Hook" Freeman, and Sheila Freeman; middle row, Verneil "Fat" Freeman and Melvin "Heavy" Freeman; back row, Jerome "Little Hook" Freeman and Larry Freeman.

The Lamb family—Gail Lamb Roddy's father, uncles, and cousins—paused for a photo during a work day in Little Rock, Arkansas, in the summer of 1971. Clockwise from left, they are Fulton Lamb (Gail's dad), Mabel Lamb, James Odell Lamb, Ellard Lamb III, Forrest Lamb, Ernest Larone Lamb, Felton Lamb, Albert Lamb Jr., Albert Lamb, Ellard Lamb II, and Ernest Lamb (popping the impressive gum bubble).

Like Bill Roddy's forebears, Fulton Lamb, Gail Lamb Roddy's father, was from rural Arkansas, where his fierce self-reliance and protectiveness of his children were forged. Here's Fulton as a young man. Fulton was a little suspicious of Bill's intention toward his daughter at first, but softened over time. Sadly, he died several years before Bill and Gail were wed.

The Grass family—Owatonna, in southern Minnesota, was a world away from the streets on the west side of Chicago where Bill Roddy grew up. Yet when Ron Grass, Bill's St. Thomas friend, took him to visit his parents, Paul and Shirley Grass, Bill felt right at home, for the values that shaped their family were the same values he had grown up with in his close-knit extended Chicago family. The Grasses, shown here in a 2009 photo, became friends for life.

Sometimes it takes perspective, of time or perhaps of distance—like that provided by Google maps in these images of Bill's old Chicago neighborhood—to see just how small and interconnected our corners of the world are. Looking back, Bill came to realize just how important the people living on those streets in his formative decades, the 1960s and '70s, were in shaping the man he is today.

After several years of friendship, Bill Roddy and Gail Lamb became husband and wife on April 13, 1990. Partners in business as well as marriage, they put their dream of helping nurture self-respect and entrepreneurship in young people into practice when they founded Osiris Organization in Minnesota in 1997.

Marcia Bach, my boss when I was the Multicultural Tennis Director at the USTA. The best boss I have ever had!

Chapter 3

In my senior year, Coach Vaughn took over the varsity team. In those days, only a certified teacher could be the coach. He was our coach on paper, but Crane's administration brought in Coach Willie White. Coach White was well known throughout the basketball community. He had coached several legends in many summer tournaments over the years. All of his teams won leagues, divisions, and championships. His knowledge of the game was impeccable. He was our version of Bobby Knight, the famous volatile coach of the University of Indiana basketball team.

I was thinking this would be the time when I would break out of my confidence slump, have a good senior year, and play guard alongside Ernest. Fink would be proud!

Coach Willie White was the most knowledgeable, demanding, and intense coach I've ever met. He knew the ins and outs of each position like the back of his hand. When he took over the team, everyone had to earn his position on the team. Our team was close; we truly cared about one another. My teammates were Ernest "E-Thang" Williams, Walter "Junior Man" Green, Ernest "Brother

Ern" Leaks, Michael "King Hoover" Lewis, Lamar "Big Dipper" Kimbrough, Willie "Griff" Griffin, Cranston Arnold, Anthony Longstreet, Glen Rodgers, Ron Jones, and Keith "Magnetic" Price.

I can recall Coach White talking to the guards about the art of playing those positions. In particular, he went into great detail about how when playing the second guard position, there was an art to creating space in order to get your shot off.

"Nag," Coach called out to me as Ernest and Walt executed guard drills, "basketball is a chess game in motion."

"You have to use your mind and intelligence to perform consistently and grow as a player," he said, beaming with excitement. "First you have to master the fundamentals, and then the sky is the limit. Becoming a great basketball player is a long process. It takes dedication and many hours of practice."

"Nag, you hear television announcers talking about black basketball players as 'athletic.' It's as if we don't have minds, are not intelligent, as if our bodies are on autopilot out of our mothers' wombs. Announcers only use 'intelligent' when describing white basketball players. Sad time in our country, Nag."

I looked at him in complete consternation. I knew the 1960s and the civil rights movement had influenced him as well. But what did that have to do with all of the stuff going on inside me?

Coach White spoke at length about how he wanted to teach us to observe and remember the defender's idiosyncrasies and weaknesses in defensive schemes. What was he talking about? I did not play chess. So what did chess have to do with anything?

I didn't make the starting five that year and lost out to sophomore Walter Green. Walt was a confident player and impressed Coach White enough to become the last starter on the team. I was disappointed, but deep down I understood and accepted his decision. In between practice bouts, Coach White would tell us inspiring stories about players he'd coached at Crane and around the community and country, including Tom "Bushwack" Bush, Willie "Nig" Williams, and many other names I don't remember. If only we'd had a tape recorder. His stories were inspiring.

Coach White was also perceptive about human nature. I remember profound remarks he made to me during my senior year. Once he called me over during a break while all the other players were getting water.

"Nag, come over here for a second."

"Yeah, Coach." Nervous, I put my hands on my hips. I was sweating bullets. Why did he single me out?

"I'm not sure why you lack confidence in yourself. You have no idea how talented you are. During practice you work harder than any player on the team," he said intensely. Then his voice took on an inspiring and respectful tone. "You are one of the most respectful young men I have ever met. One day when you resolve what's bothering you inside, you will be unstoppable. You will make a wonderful husband to a very deserving young lady."

I felt truly touched by his sincerity. His tone of voice and his penetrating focus on my eyes sent chills through me. He and I both knew there was something going on inside of me, but neither one of us had any answers. As respectfully as I could, I said, "Thanks, Coach," and we continued practice. Nothing else was ever said about it. It was one of those moments I've never forgotten.

I played a little coming off the bench that year, mainly as a substitute at forward and guard position to allow Ernest or Walt to rest. They were playing great together at the guard positions, and the team did well under Coach White.

I would wonder, "Why am I receiving all Coach's insights at this time in my life?" He imparted most of those insights during practice breaks. I've often wondered through the years how he sensed the conflict inside of me. Did he have an Aunt Sam or Aunt Betty who had counseled him when *he* was young? Why did he tell me that I would become a good husband instead of a future NBA player? Another one of life's mysteries.

Coach Vaughn attended some of our practices with Coach White to help out. I bonded quickly with Coach Vaughn on the sidelines. He never said a demeaning word to me, but was very encouraging. He reminded me of my grandfather and Ernest.

Most of the athletes at Crane gravitated to Coach Vaughn because he was the varsity football coach. He was a no-nonsense type who let you know where you stood. His mere presence commanded respect.

I wasn't the only player Coach Willie White talked to during our practice breaks. He seemed to sense when one of us needed his guidance. I wondered, and still wonder, how his guidance affected the rest of my teammates. What did he say to *them*? Did it affect them as much as it did me?

Aunt Betty and I continued to have our late-night talks. We sat and listened to R&B songs on the radio. She tried to teach me some dance moves for our upcoming senior prom, but I had two left feet. She told me many stories; some are vague memories, but some are as clear as looking out a window on a sunny day.

Aunt Betty was the first to talk to me about my biological father. She told me that his name was Larry Woodson and that he lived in a southern suburb of Chicago. She told me I should at least meet him. She said everyone had called him "Butch" when they were all in high school in Marvell. She thought he was a good person.

Aunt Betty never suggested that I aspire to become a doctor, lawyer, teacher, or member of any particular profession. She would say the kinds of things Aunt Ida often said, but in different ways.

"Daddy and Mama wanted all of us to use education to better ourselves." Aunt Betty looked thoughtful as she continued. "So what you do with that education is up to you. But he never saw you becoming a big-time professional athlete."

I had no reply, no understanding to bring any clarity to this insightfulness, but her words were stored in my mind. The understanding came much later.

During my junior and senior years, I participated in the school's student employment program, a collaboration between downtown businesses and inner-city schools. Its purpose was to provide employment to high school juniors and seniors. We received credits toward graduation for attending the program and had to make satisfactory progress in all of our other classes at school in order to continue participating in it. Ms. Loving, the director, did a great job of getting jobs for the students. I worked in the early mornings from 7 to 11 a.m. and would arrive back at school around noon each day.

Sometimes I went straight to Ms. Loving's office and let her know how things were going on the job assignment. We made lots of small talk. She told me that she lived in a southern suburb called Markham. I told her that I was thinking about trying to contact my biological father, who at the time was living in Harvey, a southern suburb near Markham. Ms. Loving said she would be willing to help me if I needed her assistance. I told her thanks but that I hadn't made up my mind yet and wasn't sure how my grandparents would feel about it.

It was the heart of the basketball season, and I didn't want any more stress on my mind. I was dealing with living in K-Town, with the conflicts and the shame of not living up to my basketball potential in a basketball-obsessed environment. My confidence was shaky at best, and I didn't have any answers. More stress? No thanks.

I constantly reflected on Coach White's statements, along with Aunt Betty's insights and her sharing of my grandfather's hopes for me. It took a statement from Coach Vaughn to bring all of the pieces together.

Ernest and Walt had become great friends off the court as well. My family and I were living in K-Town, while Ernest was still living in our old community. I took the bus home most days after practice. I did my homework if I had any, or just went to the playground and played basketball with Romero, the gang members, and the locals.

Was I jealous of Ernest's relationship with Walt? Honestly? No. I had too much on my mind at the time. I liked being alone in my bedroom in the evening to think things over. Ernest and I had a bond that could never be broken. The amount of time we spent together was not important. What we talked about when we were together was more important than the amount of time we spent together. I knew he would be a great friend to Walt, and I truly hoped Walt would see, feel, and accept what I felt while being with Ernest. In a military battle, Ernest would have been one of the guys you wanted by your side.

As the season progressed, some of the team members skipped some of their classes. When Coach Vaughn found out, he asked Coach Willie White to gather the team together during a practice break. I remember that day as if it were yesterday. I looked into Coach's eyes, sensing that something very important was about to happen. But I had no idea of the magnitude of what was about come out of his mouth.

"I know some of you are skipping classes, but you are only

short-changing yourselves," he told us. "You will need more than basketball in your lives. You will need your education to make it in this world."

The final portion of Coach Vaughn's speech is what resonated most with me.

> "Let basketball be a vehicle that you can use to improve your life by taking you to places you only dreamt of. Use basketball, but don't let basketball use you."

Later that week we found out that several teachers had approached Coach Vaughn. They told him which players were skipping classes. Most of the teachers were concerned about the student athletes' education. They knew Coach Vaughn was equally concerned. Teachers *and* coaches worked together to help us mature and succeed. Both were educators and knew it would take more than our basketball skills for us to make it in society.

At that moment, basketball took on a whole new meaning.

Coach's statement was the culmination. It helped me understand my commitment to my grandparents' values. What my grandparents had expressed to me directly had now been confirmed by Aunt Betty, Aunt Sam, Aunt Ida, school teachers, and coaches. Coach's statement was all that I needed to hear at that moment in my life. I felt his passion, his love for us, his disappointment in the few who were skipping classes as if it were the whole team doing it. It felt like he was talking to me personally. I felt a sense of calm. Some of the players got it, and some didn't.

For instance, we all knew that Walt was struggling with his classes mainly because he wasn't attending most of them. He was very intelligent but easily distracted, and eventually he became ineligible for the remainder of the season. Later, he did attend college in Wisconsin and play on his college basketball team. Whenever I talk to Ernest these days, he always updates me on our good friend Walt.

I played point guard; my natural position was off guard/ shooting guard. Ernest was a natural shooter as well, and I gladly accepted my role at the point position.

I remember the last game of the regular reason against Harrison High School, another West Side school. Our team had played well in our previous five games, but against Harrison, I made two crucial turnovers that I felt cost us the game.

I was so disappointed in myself. I had let the team down during a critical time. I could see the disappointment in Coach White's face. Even though I had resolved my internal conflicts, I still felt ashamed of my performance. The point guard position is a reflection of the coach on the floor. I represented my coach, my high school, and its reputation, and I had failed when the team needed me most. We still made the playoffs. We won the first two playoff games and eventually lost to the state champions, Wendell Phillips High School.

Students who attended inner-city Chicago games had great school spirit and would direct taunts at the opposing teams. After Wendell Phillips had the game wrapped up and during the closing minutes, all of the people on their side of the stands chanted the words to a popular Ohio Players song, "It's all over, it's over, it's over now." They chanted for several minutes. They let us know we were done.

Sometimes it's through our failures and disappointments that we learn about aspects of ourselves. I have often reflected on the Harrison game and learned to use that experience as a motivating factor and not let it define who I am as a person.

Even when I felt the shame and disappointment that

accompanied that loss, I knew it was not a reflection of me as a whole. That game was one of the best things to happen to me. It made me stronger.

It taught me to learn from all of life's experiences. We human beings seem to understand and grow more through fear and pain than we do through love—another one of life's ironies, it seems to me. Later in life I learned that it doesn't have to be that way.

Chapter 4

Coach Vaughn resigned from Crane and moved his family to Minneapolis, Minnesota. Coach White had promised to help us get into colleges. But after basketball season ended, he moved on with other things in his life. We were left to take care of applying for college ourselves.

I knew that my life in Chicago was ending. Somehow I was able to get Coach Vaughn's contact information in Minneapolis. I called him immediately.

"Hi, Coach Vaughn, this is Nag calling."

"Hey Nag, how are you doing?" Coach sounded so upbeat.

"Not so good, Coach. Coach White was unable to help us get into college. We had a few local junior colleges express interest, but I want to leave Chicago. I was wondering if you could contact some of the colleges in Minnesota and ask if they need any players?"

"OK, Nag," he said, his voice first resonating concern, then, a take-charge tone. "Let me put a call in to Coach Bill Musselman at the University of Minnesota. I will get back to you within a few days."

He knew Coach Musselman because one of our high school teammates, James Jackson, had been recruited by the University of Minnesota in 1974.

Coach Vaughn called me back within a week and said Musselman had given him the names of three local colleges: Macalester College, Hamline University, and the College of St. Thomas, all in St. Paul, Minnesota. Coach Vaughn said he had put calls in to all three coaches but had not yet heard from them.

"Once I hear from them I will arrange for a few of you guys to come up and meet the coaches," he said. "All three of these schools are strong academically. These are private universities that don't give out athletic scholarships. You should be able to qualify for some financial aid if accepted."

"OK, thanks, Coach."

I prepared to leave my family for the first time in my life. They were very happy for me. I was eighteen and was ready for the next exciting phase in my life. Amazingly, I started feeling calm and could not understand why. I told a few of the players that I had contacted Coach Vaughn and that they were welcome to go to Minnesota with me. The only one showing any interest was Ernest "E-Thang" Williams, who had played forward for our team and was an incredible rebounder.

May 1975. Coach Vaughn called and said he heard back from the coach at the College of St. Thomas (now the University of St. Thomas) in St. Paul.

"Their coach would like you to come up and work out with some of his players," he said. "When can you come up?"

"Coach, I will start working on the funds to take the bus and ask a few other players to see if they have an interest," I replied. "Can we stay with you while we're there, Coach?"

"Absolutely, you can. I think you will like Minnesota."

My sense of calm was strengthened. For the first time, I felt peace. I was headed to a place that supported some of my family values, a small private university that had no athletic scholarships, that emphasized education, where sports was a distant second, and where there would be no more pie-in-the-sky conversations about ultimately playing NBA basketball!

I had never revealed my internal conflicts to Aunt Betty, but she could tell that I had something going on inside. It was our late-night conversations, after her kids had gone to bed, that had helped me realize that my dedication to our family values was the right direction to take. I was coming to realize that basketball would be a stepping stone toward something else, but I still had no idea what that would be.

During my senior year at Crane, Aunt Betty, Coach White, and Coach Vaughn, and my friendship with Ernest, had been catalysts moving me into manhood, a process my grandfather had lovingly and firmly started.

I can still hear Coach Vaughn's affirmation: *Use basketball, but don't let basketball use you.*

I knew my grandparents could not afford to send me to college. So using basketball as a vehicle to get to college made sense to me. Basketball now took on a whole new and *constructive* meaning!

I asked E-Thang, "Hey man, you still interested in coming with me to check out the school in Minnesota?"

"Yeah, Nag, let's check it out!"

Coach Vaughn picked us up at the Greyhound bus station in downtown Minneapolis. He mentioned how clean Minneapolis was, how high its quality of life was, and asked how the other players were doing back in Chicago. The St. Thomas coach had arranged for us to work out with several current and former players at the college the following day.

"You guys want to see some of the city before we get to my house?"

This was akin to asking kids if they wanted to visit a candy store! "*Yeah*, Coach."

He drove around the parks and lakes of south Minneapolis. E-Thang and I could not believe how clean the city was in comparison to Chicago.

"Nag, it looks like one big suburb, don't it?" E-Thang remarked.

Seeing the lakes and parks was all that I needed. At that moment, my mind was made up: If I got into this school in St. Paul, Minneapolis' twin city, this is where I wanted to live.

When we arrived at Coach Vaughn's home that evening, his wife, son, and daughter warmly welcomed us.

The next morning we arrived on the campus of St. Thomas. Coach Tom Feely greeted us and thanked Coach Vaughn for contacting him. Waiting in the gym were several of his current and former players. He matched E-Thang and I with one of his former players, John Morin, a.k.a. "Lou."

We played three-on-three games for 45 minutes or more. E-Thang and I did extremely well and enjoyed displaying our skills. We wanted to make Coach Vaughn proud of us.

An opportunity to leave Chicago, to be close to Coach Vaughn, and to be in an atmosphere where the prevailing values were similar to those of my family? In my young mind, it just didn't get any better than that.

After our workout, I could see the excitement on Coach Vaughn's face, but Coach Feely was almost drooling with excitement. He asked us to commit on the spot. He also made it clear that academics at St. Thomas were taken very seriously. We had showed Coach Feely that we could make the grade on the basketball court. Now he told us we had to make the academic grades, too, to be accepted. This was Division III basketball, and if we decided to attend, we would have to be serious in the classroom.

He took us on a tour of the campus and introduced us to some of the other coaches. We stopped by the admissions office and picked up enrollment applications to take back to Chicago. Coach Vaughn mentioned to Coach Feely that we would be in town for a few more days and would be spending time with James Jackson at the University of Minnesota.

Coach Feely asked if we wanted to go and see the Minnesota Twins play. E-Thang didn't show any interest, but I said yes. The next day Coach Vaughn dropped me off on campus and Coach Feely and I attended a Twins game at the old Metropolitan Stadium in Bloomington.

Coach Feely had contacted alumnus Mike Casey, who worked for the Minnesota Twins organization. Mike had arranged for us to sit in the booth with his father, Bob Casey, the Twins' longtime public address announcer. Bob's booth was right next to that of Twins owner Calvin Griffith.

I immediately thought of my grandfather, and knew he would have been thrilled to watch a game from the public address announcer's booth. Flashes and memories of our conversations at the White Sox games poured back.

As a young man, certainly I was impressed with our seats at the game, but my mind was already made up about attending St. Thomas if I was accepted. During the game Coach Feely and I talked about the importance of education, family values, working hard, and the contacts I could make in college that would last a lifetime. When he talked about his wife and kids and his voice grew passionate, he reminded me of Coach Willie White.

Coach Feely asked me what other colleges Coach Vaughn had contacted.

"Macalester and Hamline were contacted, but you were the only one to return Coach Vaughn's phone call," I said. "Coach, if they call, I will tell them that I've already made my decision on attending St. Thomas." Coach Feely smiled with excitement, and so did I.

During our conversation that hot August afternoon at the Twins baseball game, the word basketball wasn't even mentioned.

How could it be possible for my grandfather and Coach Feely

to have similar values? They came from different worlds and were raised in totally different environments. Did similar values transcend racial, economic, political, religious views and social barriers? What was it about family values that caused us to seek out others like ourselves? Was such seeking a verification and validation of those values? Or was it just a trait wired into our DNA that compelled us to desire a sense of belonging to one another?

The next day, E-Thang, Coach Vaughn, and I visited the University of Minnesota in Minneapolis to spend time with James Jackson, the Crane High recruit from the previous year. James was happy to see us and showed us around Williams Arena and his dorm. He introduced us to Mychal Thompson, Osborne Lockhart, and one of the assistant coaches, Jimmy Williams.

Afterward, at Coach Vaughn's home, we talked in detail about our experience. I told Coach Vaughn that I wanted to attend St. Thomas if accepted. I could sense that E-Thang had bigger plans. I knew he wanted to go to a bigger school, a Division I or II school where basketball was more intensely promoted. But I knew in my heart that I wanted nothing to do with Division I or II basketball. E-Thang said, "Yeah, Nag, I can see you at St. Thomas; it's a better fit for you." Slowly, my internal conflicts were being resolved, and I felt very calm and happy once I had made my decision to attend St. Thomas.

Upon leaving Minnesota, Coach Vaughn said, "Nag, make sure you get in touch with Heavy to see if he would like to come along with you if you get accepted."

"OK, Coach, as soon as I get back I will get in touch with him."

Getting accepted by St. Thomas was my primary goal. Sometimes friends are more perceptive than they realize. E-Thang knew St. Thomas was the place for me!

Back in Chicago, the first thing I did was complete all the enrollment forms and mail them to Coach Feely. I contacted Heavy and told him about my trip to Minnesota, about being with Coach Vaughn and visiting the College of St. Thomas.

Coach Vaughn and Heavy were very close. Heavy had played junior varsity for Coach Vaughn during his freshman year at Crane. Heavy had attended several local colleges and now was living back at home in our old community.

I'd never had a direct conversation with Heavy. He was three years older than me (at that age, a difference that felt like light years), so he was out of my reach during my middle school and high school years.

Heavy was one of the legends in our community and at Crane High School. Junior varsity and varsity basketball teams traveled together on the buses to all away games, so Heavy knew me by sight, but not once had we ever had a one-on-one conversation.

We finally made contact, and I met with him. We made small talk for a few minutes. I told Heavy that Coach Vaughn had asked me to contact him about my experiences in Minnesota. I told him that if I got accepted, I was attending St. Thomas.

Heavy asked several questions about Minnesota, the coach at St. Thomas, and scholarships. I told him that St. Thomas was a private university and did not give out athletic scholarships. I had an extra application and gave it to him. Heavy called Coach Vaughn, and later he decided to apply.

Chapter 5

J une 1975. I was about to graduate from high school and shared with my family the possibility that I might go off to college in Minnesota.

I was also preparing emotionally to leave Chicago. I met Ms. Loving in her office one afternoon.

"Ms. Loving, are you still willing to help me contact my biological father, who is living in Harvey?"

"Absolutely," she said. "Just give me his first and last name and I will start right away. By the way, what college are you attending after graduation?"

"I just returned from looking at a school in Minnesota," I said. "If I get accepted, that's where I will go. Coach Vaughn lives in Minnesota, and I hope to hear from the college coach soon."

After graduation in June, all the basketball players asked each other about our plans. What colleges, if any, were we going to attend? I told them I hoped to attend a college in Minnesota. We all promised to stay in touch. I knew all I had to do was stay in touch with Ernest. He was the point person and would keep in touch with everyone else.

During the latter part of June I had lots of time to reflect on the possibility that I might soon be leaving my family for the first time. The thought of leaving my grandparents, Aunt Betty, Aunt Ida, and Aunt Sam, of not even being able to spend weekends with Sam, tempered my excitement with profound sadness.

I felt guilty about leaving my aunt's kids. They looked up to me. I tormented myself.

Am I depriving these kids of a mentor and role model?

Who will help Juan learn to throw a curve ball like my grandfather taught me?

Who will help them with their homework in the evenings like Aunt Ida did for me?

Who will babysit the kids while Aunt Ida and Aunt Betty go out some weekends after working hard all week?

Will I been able to survive without Aunt Yam's hugs?

After college, what will my life be like?

My aunts had dedicated so much time, energy, and nurturing to me during my formative years while simultaneously raising their own kids. To them, I was nephew and son at the same time.

It was an exciting time for me, but also one loaded with guilt about college taking me away from my mentoring role.

July 1975. I got a call from Coach Tom Feely. "Hi, Billy. You got accepted, along with Melvin." I was so excited that I could hardly speak.

"Thanks for calling, Coach! I will contact Melvin and let him know. We will try to come to Minnesota a little early to get situated on campus."

"Ok, Billy. Congratulations on being accepted! Call me when you have your exact dates of your arrival to St. Paul. I want to help you get situated in the dorms."

I immediately told my Aunt Betty. She was thrilled.

After several days of thinking about meeting my biological father, I had decided to call him.

"Hello," a female voice answered the phone.

"May I speak with Larry, please?"

"May I ask who is calling?"

"Yes, please tell him this is William Roddy."

"Larry, there is a William Roddy on the phone."

A pause. Then: "This is Larry speaking."

"Hi Larry, this is William Roddy. You know my aunts: Betty, Ida, Samella, and Rosella. They are Irene's younger sisters. They have mentioned your name to me for many years. Aunt Betty was the one who encouraged me to contact you."

It felt like an hour passed before he replied.

"I have often wondered how you were doing," he said. "I never wanted to disturb your life or disrespect your grandparents while they were raising you. I never knew how they might feel about me being in your life. Your mother and I were so young when you were born. I am glad to hear from you, and would love to meet you."

I was stunned speechless for a moment.

"I would love to meet you as well, because next month I am leaving to go to college in Minnesota," I said.

We arranged to meet. After our phone conversation, I informed Aunt Betty that I had made contact with my biological father, the man she called Butch.

"How did the conversation go?" she asked.

"He was very nice to talk to over the phone," I said. "He said he was looking forward to meeting me. We set up a meeting for next Saturday afternoon."

Butch's home, Saturday afternoon. His wife answered the door and invited me in. She ushered me into their living room, then went to get Butch. My heart raced. I was so nervous. What if he didn't like me? Why was his wife looking at me like that? Was this a big mistake?

As Butch entered the living room, we made eye contact. He immediately smiled at me, and I returned one to him. We shook hands and said hi. I felt a warm sensation and saw a loving reflection in his eyes. But when his wife sat down with us, I felt uneasy. I sensed she was not happy that I was there. I could see that look in her eyes: *Why is he contacting my husband after all these years? What the hell does he want from us?*

The first few moments were uncomfortable, and I could tell that Butch sensed it as well. He asked her if she could get us something to drink. She brought back water and sodas, then returned to the kitchen. *I am glad she didn't join us,* I thought. *Apparently she got the hint.*

"What do your grandparents call you?" he asked.

"They all call me Little Henry because I'm named after my grandfather," I said. "But mostly they just call me Lil for short.

"Would it be OK if I call you Lil? How did you find me?"

"Yes, you can call me Lil. Aunt Betty knew your first and last name. My work program director at Crane High School lives in Markham and helped me find your number in the Harvey phonebook."

"Oh, I remember Betty. Your work program director obviously thought enough of you to help with contacting me," he said. "I can already see your grandparents and aunts did a great job raising you. I know they are proud of you."

He was soft spoken. He stood about 5 feet 8. He had a warm smile that complemented his gentle eyes. I wondered, *Do I look like him? What features do we share?* People have often told me I have Irene's jaw line and mouth. But I could see that I had Larry's eyes. I loved his eyes!

Then he began to talk about something more personal.

"I owe you an explanation of why I haven't been in touch with you," he said. He lowered his eyes just a bit. "I never wanted to interfere in your life. I wanted to respect your grandparents. I knew you would be loved and well taken care of. John Albert, your cousin, kept me posted on your life. Many years have passed, and the past is the past. I would be happy if we could start a friendship with one another from this moment on."

"I would like that," I said. "My Aunt Betty remembers some of the times back in Arkansas when all of you were young in middle and high school."

"Yes, I remember all of your aunts very well. Your grandfather was a proud and respectable man while living in Arkansas. So you went to Crane High School and now you're going to college?"

"Yes, my grandfather's values are how we live our lives. I am happy being accepted into college. I just wanted to meet you before I leave in August. It's a small private college in St. Paul, Minnesota, the College of St. Thomas. I plan to major in business and will play on the basketball team."

"That's great," he said. "I know your grandparents and aunts will be sad and happy about you leaving."

"Yes, I think they probably will be sad for a while," I said. "I owe them everything. Together, they all raised me and taught me a lot."

"When are you leaving for college?"

"Last week in August."

"In July and August, I have several weeks of vacation time left. I would love to spend time with you before you leave. I work at the Ford Motor Company plant in Indiana. I have been there for over twenty-five years. I would love to show it to you sometime. I also have a cabin in South Haven, Michigan. My wife and I will be going there in August. Maybe you could join us?" His eyes seemed to light up.

"That would be great. May I call you early next week to set up a time to meet?"

"Absolutely. I look forward to seeing you again."

"May I call you Larry?"

"You can me Larry, Lawrence, or Butch. I am glad you contacted me!"

"I like 'Larry.'"

I rose to leave. Larry asked for my phone number. We agreed to make contact early the next week. He and his wife stood on their front steps and waved goodbye.

I knew that I was an intruder in his wife's life and that she would be much happier if I never returned. It was not what she said; it was her body language and the looks she gave me. But I sensed something completely different from Larry. If I had sensed that negative vibe from him, I would not have contacted him again.

I thought of Aunt Sam. She had taught me one of the most valuable skills in life, learning to read another person's body language to be able to tell if they accepted or rejected you. She taught me this skill without so much as ever saying a word.

Later in life I realized that my Aunt Sam knew her life's purpose very young, long before self-help books on finding your life's purpose were ever written. Without even knowing it, she was our family's spiritual and emotional healer. Or perhaps Aunt Sam did know this and it led her to nurture us all?

I turned the ignition in my grandfather's car and drove around the corner out of sight of Larry and his wife. Emotions flooded me. I knew I was not in a position to drive at that moment. I sat in the car for about ten minutes before I left.

My mind raced. Among my thoughts:

Glad I followed Aunt Betty's encouragement to meet Larry.

I can tell Larry is a good person, like she said.

I know his wife wishes I would never return.

Ms. Loving's statements about taking it slow were good advice. I need to thank her.

If I continue my relationship with Larry, will this affect his relationship with his wife in a negative way?

Was Larry surprised? How does he feel right now? Does he feel a sense of guilt for not being a part of my formative years?

What did he sense from me? What was he expecting? Was he reading my thoughts and sensing my emotions as I tried to do the same to him?

Did we connect?

I had finally met the other person responsible for bringing me into the world. The thought brought tears to my eyes that afternoon as I sat in my grandfather's Ford. I had connected with an important missing piece of a puzzle. Many years later, I would realize what a wonderful healing event this was for me.

Now the real work would start—dealing with everyone's responses and questions, especially my grandparents'.

I don't remember the drive home. It was all a blur. All I remember is taking the steps two at a time as I ran up to talk to Aunt Betty, my wise and loving counselor.

I was so excited as I entered the first floor of the duplex where my grandfather, grandmother, and I lived and gave him the keys to his Ford. He said they were going to the store to get some groceries and would be back in an hour.

I raced upstairs looking for Aunt Betty. Words did not come out right as I approached her. She was in the kitchen preparing food for her kids and a couple of our neighbor's kids. (One tenet of our family values was to never turn away kids when it was time to eat. When we were young, my grandfather forbade us to eat at someone else's home. But neighborhood kids were free to eat at our table. Go figure.)

"Aunt Betty, I need to talk to you." I was breathless and excited.

"Lil, slow down; we got lots of time to talk. Let me finish cooking the food for the kids."

"Do you want me to help you with anything?"

"Yes, get the dishes and silverware out and put them on the table. The food will be ready in about five minutes."

Those five minutes seemed like an hour. As I looked around the table at my cousins and neighbor kids, I realized that they were far more important than my urgency to share my story. Aunt Betty kept me in the moment.

Finally it was time to tell my story.

"Aunt Betty, Larry is everything you said he was," I told her. "We talked about meeting again next week. He remembers all of us in Arkansas. We talked about developing a friendship, about not feeling bad, angry, or guilty about the past. He said the past is the past and we can't change it. He asked if we could start a new relationship from this moment on."

I must have been babbling a mile a minute, but Aunt Betty calmly listened to every word.

"Lil, I am glad your first meeting went good," she said. "I had to let Mama and Daddy know that you were meeting with Butch. I will continue to support your developing a relationship with him. I told Mama and Daddy that I was the one to encourage you to meet him."

I was speechless at first. "What did they say?"

"Daddy didn't say anything, but Mama wants to talk to you."

"I just dropped the car keys off with Daddy, and he didn't say anything."

"Did you see Mama?" she asked, hesitantly.

"No, she was getting dressed, and I just wanted to talk to you right away."

What I feared most was facing my grandmother. I remember how, when I had skipped classes my junior year at Crane, I had faced her wrath and disappointment. And when she thought my grandfather was disrespected, she would turn into a verbal warrior in his defense, letting the offending party or parties know that they had violated something sacred.

The wait for my grandparents to return from the store seemed like a whole day instead of an hour. That was way too much idle time for me to deal with. Finally, Aunt Betty and I heard the downstairs door open on the first level of our duplex. They had arrived home from grocery shopping.

"Lil, you better go down and help them unload the groceries."

"OK, are you and Aunt Ida going out tonight?" I knew I would probably need reinforcements later in the evening.

"No, we don't get paid until next weekend, so we will go out next weekend. I got lots of clothes to wash and cleaning to do." She seemed a little tired; regardless, I knew she'd support me in every way.

"May I come up and talk to you later?"

"Yes, and you can help wash some clothes, too."

I went downstairs to my grandparents' living quarters. They were putting groceries into the refrigerator. They didn't say much, just made small talk about the deals they had gotten at the store and what they were going to cook for the evening meal.

"Hi, Mama and Daddy, do you want me to help with the groceries?"

"No, we're almost done, but take all the bags on the table and put them in the garbage," Daddy said.

My grandmother didn't say a word to me.

Daddy turned to leave the room. "I'm going into the living room to watch those sorry-ass White Sox," he said. "Their pitching staff is the worst in the American League. They are playing a doubleheader tonight."

"I bet that sorry-ass Wilbur Wood is on the mound tonight for the first game. I could throw a knuckleball better than he can with my damn left hand," he said, his voice now raised to a roar. He turned to me and asked, "Do you want to watch the game with me after you talk to your grandmother?"

"Aunt Betty would like me to help with some work a little later. I will watch the second game later tonight with you."

My grandmother slammed the refrigerator door. "Lil Henry,

come here. I need to talk to you about something."

I suddenly wished I could disappear from the face of the Earth for about a week. I knew what was coming. There was nothing in the world I could do but listen and keep quiet until she finished.

"Betty said you got in touch with Butch," she said, her eyes blazing. "What the hell has he ever done for you? Henry and me decided to raise you after you were born for reasons unknown to you. Irene was too young to take care of you. We did not know how Butch would treat you. They were very young. Later Irene got married to Osbe Sr. and moved to Michigan. The thought of you going to some unknown place was too much for us. Henry and I thought it would be best if we raised you with us in Arkansas. Henry did not trust any other man raising you, and I didn't either."

I hung my head.

"Why in the hell did you feel the need to contact him?" she demanded. "Did we do something wrong? Was Butch around to change your shitty diapers, take you to kindergarten, buy you clothes to wear for school, stay up late when you were sick, or put bandages on your ass when you fell down from playing outside?"

Aunt Betty once told me that many people had their opinions of Butch. My grandmother definitely had hers. I was brought before the court; my grandmother, in full-blown warrior princess mode, was the judge, juror and the executioner that afternoon. Disrespecting my grandparents? Mama made it clear I was guilty as charged.

Grandfather was in the background screaming at the television. "*Damn*, man! Swing the bat! It's called baseball! These young guys are getting paid lots of money. Hell, I can stand at the plate, watch the ball go by, and hope for a walk!"

Balled out by my grandmother, I skulked straight to my room. As I passed my grandfather, he asked if I was done talking to Mama. I said yes, and continued on to my room and closed the door. He knew I needed to be alone.

"Why are the White Sox keeping Wilbur Wood in the starting

rotation? His ERA is higher than a damn kite." Daddy raved on for about five minutes straight. I put on my headphones to drown out his armchair commentary. Led Zeppelin and Yes actually sounded soothing after my grandmother's sermon.

Lying in my bed that evening, I thought about going upstairs to talk to Aunt Betty. But I decided being alone was best.

I never got a chance to explain to my grandmother the conversation Larry and I had. I just accepted grandmother's guilty verdict. Nothing else I could do.

After meeting Butch for the first time, I was able to form my own opinion of him. I felt, though, that I still shouldn't argue with my grandparents' guilty verdict—for him and me. After all, I was living in their home.

So that day I was catapulted back into my role as a chastised child. Transitioning into manhood was temporarily on hold. I was done for the day. My grandparents were still the law.

Chapter

One of the most touching moments that summer came on a Saturday morning in August. I knew that Aunt Betty had told my grandparents I would soon be attending college in Minnesota. We all knew the time had arrived for me to leave the nest.

I met my grandfather on our front porch. He was sitting there watching the cars go up and down Jackson Boulevard. This was rare because he was always up and about, working around the house on some little project.

"Daddy, I got accepted into college in Minnesota and will be leaving at the end of the month," I said.

He didn't directly look at me, but clearly he was listening. I told him how excited I was that I soon would be entering a new environment at college and meeting students from all over the world, and how much I looked forward to playing on the basketball team.

"I know; Betty told me," he said. "Son, I have done all that I can do for you. Be the best man you can be. I will always be proud of you, and *I love you.*"

It was the first time in my life my grandfather had ever said the word "love" to me. I'd never even heard him tell my grandmother that he loved her, although we all knew that he did.

I was shocked. Tears welled in my eyes. As respectfully as I could, I responded, "Daddy, I love you, *too*!"

Suddenly he said, "I need your help to fix that garage door again. I think we need to put some new hinges on it or just replace the whole door."

"OK, Daddy, when do you want to do it?"

"Let's do it this evening. I want to watch the Sox game this afternoon." He went on and on about how he could help the White Sox win if they would only listen to him. How I loved him!

Men of his generation rarely verbally expressed affection. Apparently they believed that words of affection demonstrated weakness and were not "manly." His utterance of the word "love" shocked me, but at the same time I knew exactly what he meant. He'd done the best job he could raising me. This was the farthest he could take me. I knew he hoped that his values were firmly planted into my young heart, mind, and soul. But only time would tell.

Our conversation that Saturday morning only lasted only a few minutes. I have often wondered what made men of his generation uncomfortable saying "love" to someone they care for? What if other men said this to their sons more often?

Could saying "I love you" make a difference in father-son relationships all over the world?

I'm certain of one thing. Hearing my grandfather say "I love you" made all the difference to *me*.

Chapter 7

On Sunday morning, my grandmother and some of Aunt Betty's and Aunt Ida's kids got ready to attend church. My grandfather would always take them to and from church.

We talked while my grandmother decided which hat and purse would complete her outfit. She asked me, as she always did, if I wanted to come to church with her. There was no mention of her previous sermon, or questions about what I thought about what she said, or about what Butch was like.

I knew she was disappointed in me for not attending church regularly with her. I did attend church once in a while with her, but I never felt inspired. My grandfather's values and my aunts' implementation of those values had inspired in me an intense introspective journey. The thought of looking outside of myself for guidance and clarity was foreign to me.

In so many ways, I was a lot like my grandfather. He did believe in a supreme being; we both did. But he never wanted anyone telling him how to live his life. I knew he thought preachers overstepped their bounds when my grandmother would occasionally invite them to our house for dinner after church.

When my grandmother invited her pastor over for dinner, she would seat him at the head of the table and serve him first. I knew my grandfather thought this was insulting to him as the head of our household. I watched him during those dinners, and I could see that it infuriated him. Knowing my grandfather, he probably had a heart-to-heart talk with my grandmother about it, because the dinner invitations soon came to a halt.

My grandfather never demanded that I attend church, nor did he discourage me from going. He left it up to me. For me, my grandfather's presence was a spiritual experience in itself.

I was preparing to leave Chicago and felt every second of my time with my grandfather was precious. I wanted to spend those last days with him and also, I hoped, to get to know Larry.

Late that Sunday morning after my grandmother and the kids had left for church, I went straight upstairs to talk to Aunt Betty.

"Hi, Aunt Betty. I had my talk with Mama yesterday."

"I know, I heard," she replied. "Are you going to meet Butch again?"

"Yes, next week he wants to take me to his job. He works at the Ford Motor plant in Indiana."

I searched her face for reassurance. She was pleased. "Good, I'm glad you will be seeing him again before you leave next month for college," she said.

I left Aunt Betty and went outside just as my grandfather returned from dropping off my grandmother at church.

"I need your help with fixing the garage door," he said. "We've been putting it off all week."

"OK, Daddy, I will meet you around the back of the house."

We met at the garage behind our duplex. I knew he had something to say. *Damn! Why not just come out with it?* I settled my mind down. I waited.

He always wore his overalls while working on his car or on

projects around the house. They were standard blues that he'd once worn on our farm. His hammer, nails, screwdriver, and tape measure were hooked on the loops on those greasy overalls. He had only one pair, and they were sacred. Did he ever allow them to be washed? I'm not sure!

"When did you say you are leaving for college?"

"I'll probably leave around the last week in August. I will see if I can stay with my former high school basketball coach, Coach Vaughn. He lives in Minnesota now. He was the one who got all of this arranged for me."

"That was really nice of him to help you. Make sure you thank him for helping you. Do you need a little money to take with you?"

"Yes, I could use a little more before I start college. I have some I saved up from the work program from Crane. Once I start college I will try to find a part-time job on campus."

"Make sure you call us if you need anything. We don't want you to be worried about anything while in college."

He turned and looked me right in the eye. "Remember what I told you on the front porch last week?"

"Yeah, I won't ever forget."

As we adjusted the hinges on the garage door, we continued to talk. The conversation went from him talking about getting a brand-new door for the garage to me going to college. Suddenly, the cat came out of the bag.

"What do you think of Butch? Here, hold this in place while I tighten the screws."

Yeah, tighten the screws all right. Time suspended. I was unprepared for this question. Not from him. We made no eye contact.

Nervousness made my hands sweat. Somehow I quickly gathered my thoughts.

"He is a nice man," I said. "I just wanted to find out for myself what type of person he was. I didn't mean any disrespect to you and Mama. Aunt Betty said many people have their opinions of him and that I needed to find out for myself."

Silence. He motioned for me to hold the hinges.

Then he said: *"Son, you are a man now. You can make your own decisions. Do what you think is best. I trust you. Just remember our conversation on the front porch."*

"Thanks, Daddy. I will always remember it."

The last few weeks in August were a blur. My grandfather and I had said our goodbyes to one another. I was now a man in his eyes. I was closing an important chapter in my young life and at the same time I didn't have a clue about what was in store for me in Minnesota. But what I had was a value system that permeated my soul and would guide me through the next four years. Little did I know that it would also guide me through many more years beyond that.

All my nicknames and their personas—Lil Henry, Nag, and Sandy—welcome to manhood!

August 1975. I spent as much time as possible with my aunts, especially Aunt Betty and her kids. I saw them often because they lived upstairs. I was busy making arrangements to fly to Minnesota, saying goodbye to Romero and the locals in K-Town, and letting Ernest "Brother Ern" Leaks know I was headed to Minnesota.

Larry and I met several times in late July through late August.

"Can I take you to the airport next week?" he asked. "From Harvey to O'Hare Airport will be about an hour-and-a-half drive. I can swing by your house on the West Side and pick you up. We would have some time to talk while driving."

"Yeah, that will be great. I will get back to you with the exact date and time of my flight."

"OK, looking forward to hearing from you."

The hardest part of leaving is saying goodbye. I called Coach Vaughn in Minnesota and arranged to stay with him for a week until we incoming freshmen could move into the dorm.

Larry and I arranged to meet at our house and drive to the airport. Betty, Ida, and Sam came to see me off. They were there with several of their kids, standing in the hallway and on our front porch, when Larry arrived and parked his car on Jackson Boulevard.

"You make sure you stay in touch with us, OK?" admonished Aunt Betty.

Juan, Aunt Betty's oldest son, said, "Lil, are you coming back home in the summer to see us?"

Minnie Yvonne, Aunt Betty's only daughter, asked, "Lil, where is Minnesota?"

Aunt Ida said in her Klingon voice, "Remember, I want to attend your graduation. Don't make me come to Minnesota to straighten you out, you hear?"

Aunt Sam gave me a hug. "Call us if you need anything!"

Emotions rushed out of me. Tears poured out of my eyes. They all watched me and hugged me. My grandmother stood in the background, smiling. Where was Daddy? I guess we had said our goodbyes fixing the garage door. He was probably in the living room screaming at the White Sox.

Larry stood patiently by his car, silently observing. I approached him; he noticed my teary eyes, grabbed my suitcases, and put them in the trunk. Aunt Betty followed me. Larry and Aunt Betty greeted each other and made small talk about seeing each other for the first time in years. I was happy to see them smile at one another. I sat in

Larry's car wiping away tears.

On the road to the airport, Larry and I talked about life in general.

"Why didn't you come to the porch and meet the rest of my family?" I asked.

"That was your moment with your family," he said. "I didn't want to intrude. I haven't met your grandparents and did not want to be disrespectful by being at their home just as you were leaving them. I knew this was stressful enough for them."

I pondered that, then said, "This is the first time I have ever left my family."

"Like I said the first time we met back in July, they all have done a great job of raising you," he said. "I am glad that you contacted me. I just want to have a long-lasting friendship with you. That's all I can ever have with you. They have already done the real work."

"Real work?"

"Yes, the real work was teaching you their values. Your grandfather's values were what I noticed the moment we met. I knew you were a respectable young man with good values by the way you presented yourself."

On the ride to the airport, I listened to him talk about his life, his values, about how meeting me had added so much enjoyment to his life.

When we arrived at O'Hare Airport, he helped me with my bags and gave them to the skycap. We had a few silent, awkward moments before I went through the gates. I could tell we had made a wonderful connection. I truly felt Larry was an important piece of the puzzle I needed to assemble to transition into manhood.

"I am glad I had the pleasure of taking you to the airport," he said. "I really enjoyed our conversation. Please stay in touch with me. If you need any help, just call me."

"I am glad, too. I will stay in touch. I will call you once I get settled in Minnesota."

We hugged and said our goodbyes that hot August day.

My grandparents' values were firmly in place. My loving aunts' nurturing had taken hold. I continued to enjoy what would be a lifelong friendship with Ernest Leaks. I had learned from Fink's influence and Coach White's and Coach Vaughn's mentoring. And now I finally had a relationship with my biological father, Larry Woodson. I felt invincible. I was ready to take on the world.

Chapter 8

My grandfather, William Henry Roddy, the oldest son of Frank and Rose Lee Jackson-Roddy, was born in 1911 in Jackson County, Newport, Arkansas. The economic environment during those times forced him to drop out of school in the sixth grade and go to work on the farm. The indignities and insults that he and other African-Americans of his generation had to endure in the rural South are unimaginable to me. To all of us, he was the patriarch of our family, with a Ph.D. in common sense.

I have often wondered: Where did he get his values? Were they passed down to him from his father and mother? Or did they develop as a survival mechanism when he lived and worked in the farming community in the rural South? Why were the conversations between him and me about those values always private? Would they have benefited others?

Did he think of me, a grandson whom he considered his only son, the one who would champion his values to the world? I had witnessed all of my aunts living by those values, which had helped implement them in their own children and in me.

I wondered if I could improve on what had been bestowed upon me.

With those values to guide me, what type of people would I attract in Minnesota? Only time would tell. I was Minnesota bound!

Chapter 9

My four years at St. Thomas were memorable largely because of the relationships I developed while there. Basketball had its place during those years, but it was far removed from my consciousness as anything more than an extracurricular activity.

At St. Thomas, there was no obsessive basketball environment to deal with, no basketball goals after graduation, and no thoughts of even playing in summer leagues.

Melvin "Heavy" Freeman and I arrived together on campus. I was entering manhood with one of our local basketball legends from Chicago in an educational environment where basketball and sports were a distant second to academics. I welcomed that. But I wondered what Heavy thought.

He was assigned to Ireland Hall and I to Dowling Hall. But Heavy and I quickly bonded and were supportive of one another.

Heavy's a funny guy and can have you laughing until you get a stomachache. He also carries himself in a very confident manner. As two of just a few African-American students on campus in the mid-1970s, we encountered ignorance on many occasions. Heavy did not tolerate ignorance and stupidity. Most students learned very quickly that he was not the type of person to approach with ignorance.

On the positive side, I remember the day Heavy met Sharon Zachary. Sharon's mother was attending an educational seminar on campus that evening, When Sharon arrived to meet up with her mother, Heavy, who was not the shy type, decided to get Sharon's "digits," as the kids would say today.

"Hey, Nag, look at the pretty young sista over there. Ooooooh *wee!*

"Aw man, I am hungry and I will meet you in the grill."

"Cool, I will be right back after I talk to her."

I met and became great friends with Dan Dietz. He was the football coach's son and a sophomore living next to us. Dan invited me to his home in White Bear Lake and persuaded me to go ice fishing with him in January. Brett Jorgensen, a pre-med student from Pacifica, California, was my roommate, and would remain a supportive roommate all four of my years at St. Thomas. We spent many long nights after studying talking about our families.

Two doors down the hall were sophomores Dave Baumgartner and Jim Eppel, accounting majors from Minnetonka, a suburb of Minneapolis. Curt Feldmeier, a pre-med senior from Philadelphia, lived next door to us.

One night in the basement where all of the recreational activities took place, I met a tall, curly haired student. Like me, he was taking a study break and looking for someone to play ping-pong with.

We introduced ourselves; he was open and approachable. I sensed something special in him.

"Hi, my name is Ron Grass."

"Hi, my name is William Roddy."

"Where are you from?"

"Chicago."

"Would you like to play some ping-pong?"

"Sure."

We played for about an hour, and eventually the subject of basketball came up.

"I will be trying out for the varsity team," Ron said.

"Oh, me too. And where are you from?"

"A little town south of here called Owatonna."

"Owa, what?"

"Owatonna. I know you have never heard of it before."

"OK, how 'bout I just call it the Big O?"

Culture shock. Ron just laughed and quickly learned that this young city kid had to give nicknames to everything.

I struggled my first semester. The amount of reading and the workload from all the classes were overwhelming. I comprehended the work; it was the volume and the high expectations that were challenging. The professors knew what they wanted from all of the students in their classes and expected them to be prepared.

Coach Feely and Doc Larry Russ, the track coach, suggested that I drop one class and take a speed-reading class at the college's student learning center to stay current with my remaining classes. They also recommended that I go to summer school to make up the credits that I would drop.

Biology was one of my classes I struggled with. I asked for a tutor-mentor, someone I could study with. Dr. Richard Meierotto, my professor, suggested a senior: Curt Feldmeier.

"Curt Feldmeier? He lives next to me in Dowling Hall."

Ron Grass and I talked about basketball practice, the next upcoming game, and our homework. Ron teased me about going down to the "Big O" with him one weekend, when I would meet his parents.

"William, next weekend I am going home to see my parents. My mother makes some great chocolate chip cookies, and she always bakes enough for me to take back to school."

"Great, just let me know and I would be happy to check out the Big O and meet your parents," I said. We eventually set a date to do so.

That January afternoon in Owatonna, it appeared as if a Hallmark Christmas card had come alive before my eyes. Snow had just fallen. I had flashbacks to Chicago, to winters during elementary and middle school years, with my friends and me pitching snowballs at one another on our way home after school.

The fresh snow seemed to have cleared the air. People walked their pets in it, and kids played in it in their driveways. Clearly, this was not Chicago; Owatonna had the scenery of a utopian environment.

Driving down to the Big O, we talked a lot about our families. I could tell right away that he had great values. He loved his parents and siblings. Entering their home, I did not know what to expect.

"Mom, this is my friend William from Chicago."

His mother was in the kitchen preparing food for the evening. She turned around and looked me directly in the eyes. She had the most loving brown eyes and a smile like my Aunt Sam's. Mrs. Grass had short, light-colored hair and a round face. She invited us to sit down at the table and fed us. It brought back memories of my grandmother, who always made sure guests were taken care of. One way of doing that was to make sure they had something to eat. Ron's mom thanked Ron for bringing me down to meet her. She treated me like I was one of her sons.

I was in a small town in southern Minnesota, and it felt like home. How could this be? Mrs. Grass' kindness confirmed my belief that values start in the home.

"Ron mentioned he was bringing a friend with him this weekend. William, it's a pleasure to meet you."

"It's a pleasure to meet you as well, Mrs. Grass."

She called in her husband and Ron's younger brothers and sisters. Mr. Grass gave me a firm handshake and welcomed me to their home. Like Ron, his older brother, Tom, was on St. Thomas' basketball team; he had remained on campus that weekend. Ron's family made me feel like I was a long-lost family member coming home from the wilderness. That day I knew Ron and I would remain lifelong friends.

"Now you make sure you come see us again," Mrs. Grass said.

"I will, Mrs. Grass, and thanks for the chocolate chip cookies."

"You are welcome. Don't let this be the last time you come down to see us."

Ron and I drove back to campus that evening. For most of the ride, we were silent. Were we both contemplating what had just happened? Was this our bonding moment? Was he wondering what his family thought of this nineteen-year-old African-American from Chicago? All I felt when I met his mother was unconditional love. In a southern Minnesota town on a snowy day, I had encountered unconditional love. I wished that my Aunt Sam could meet Mrs. Grass.

To this day, when Ron goes homes to the Big O, he always brings chocolate chip cookies back for me from Mrs. Grass. Of course, they taste great, because they are made with unconditional love by an angel!

At St. Thomas, we had our regular daily routine, attending classes from 9 a.m. to 2:45 p.m. and basketball practice from 3 to 5 p.m., rushing to eat from 5:15 to 6 p.m. and heading to the library from 6:30 to 11 p.m. Monday through Thursday and Sunday to study. On Friday and Saturday, we had fun!

One day I heard loud knocking on my door. It was Curt Feldmeier.

"Dr. Richard Meierotto mentioned that you requested a tutor. Oh, by the way, great game last night. You guys played great. How did you learn to play basketball like that? Most freshmen don't play that much, but you are really talented."

Here I was looking to get help in biology and all this young future doctor wanted to do was talk basketball. Damn! I listened patiently to him for several minutes, and then thanked him for contacting me.

"Curt, I am glad you enjoyed the game last night, but I could really use your help in biology."

"OK, Billy, what can I do to help you?"

I described my challenges, and within an hour he had explained my entire biology 101 class. We went from talking about biology, to family, to basketball. He was patient and caring. I knew he would be a great doctor. He listened extremely well after he came down from his basketball high.

I was a young African-American student on an almost entirely white college campus. Why were people I had never met before reinforcing my family values? Why was I experiencing this? Was this the essence of college?

Chapter

After my freshman year, I went home to Chicago. Before I left campus, Coach Feely and I had a long talk. Like many people on campus, he called me Billy.

"Billy, I know you had a tough freshman year, but you passed all of your classes and did well on the court as well. Are you coming back?"

"Yeah, I'm coming back, Coach. It was tough adjusting to a new environment, but there is nothing in Chicago for me but my family. I am committed to staying and graduating. My family expects me to graduate, and I can't let them down."

"That's great, Billy. Why don't you come back early and we can get you into summer school and help you look for summer employment? By the way, take a break from basketball for the summer when you return."

"OK, Coach, I probably will stay in Chicago for only about two weeks and then return."

"Make sure you call me when you are about to return."

I called my Aunt Betty and informed her that I was coming home for a few weeks.

May 1976. I arrived in Chicago for the summer. It turned into the ultimate chapter-closing experience for me.

Chapter 11

The first few days home were pretty laid back. After having taken my last rounds of finals at St. Thomas, I was in need of a mental break.

But that summer, I started to see the environment in which I had spent my high school years from a strange new perspective. I could hardly believe this is where I had lived so many years. I seemed to see every minute detail of the community with heightened senses.

Among my thoughts:

How did I survive this environment?

I'm deeply saddened that I will be leaving my family again.

I wish I could take all of my aunts' kids back to Minnesota with me.

I wish they could see the quality of life in Minnesota.

Are they aware that the streets of Chicago are filthy, that there is litter all over the place? Does anyone care?

Does anyone care about the condition of their properties?

Why would they let their homes deteriorate like this?

I felt guilty for having these thoughts about my neighborhood, my neighbors.

Was I becoming a snob?

Later that week I was upstairs spending time with Aunt Betty's and Aunt Ida's kids. Aunt Sam arrived late that afternoon with her three sons. She approached me, looking directly into my eyes. She greeted me with a loving hug. It was so wonderful to see her. We talked for a while.

Aunt Sam is about the same height as my grandmother with shoulder-length black hair, dark eyes, and a smile that could stop wars. Her voice was gentle, comforting.

"Lil, what's wrong? You look sad."

I was stunned that she noticed, and poured out my thoughts.

"Aunt Sam, everything seems to be so different and horrible. I don't even want to go outside."

"Lil, everything is the same. It's you that is different. We all knew it would be hard for you to come back to Chicago once you left."

I had nothing else to say. She hugged me, and I cried in her arms.

"Lil, don't worry, everything will be OK. Just keep doing well in school; we all want to attend your graduation."

"OK, Aunt Sam." Oh, how she could calm me with a simple hug.

She went to the kitchen to talk to Aunt Betty. I stayed in the living room. Some of Aunt Betty's kids had observed and heard the conversation between Aunt Sam and me. As I dried my teary eyes, I looked up and saw that the kids were watching me. Should I do the manly thing and say everything was OK and act like nothing had happened? I told them I was OK, just feeling sad. I assured them not to worry. They all said OK and went outside to play with their friends. I stayed inside and just watched the cars pass down Jackson Boulevard.

A few days later, some of Aunt Betty's kids told Romero's younger brothers that I was home for the summer from college. Romero came over to talk to me.

"Hey Lil, how did your first year go?"

"It went OK," I said. "I struggled a little with some of my classes. It was tough being away from my family the first few months."

"Did you miss K-Town? Don't you remember me telling you, 'Ain't shit here but trouble?'"

"Yeah, I remember." And it was painful now to witness how his admonishment had been spot-on.

"It's getting worse day by day. Are you going back to Minnesota?"

"Yeah, I am, and I will look for work while attending summer school to stay on top of my credits."

"Do you want to go down to the playground and school some of those young dudes who think they can play?"

"Man, I just want to stay home with my family for a while. I played so much basketball during the season I don't want to see a basketball for a while."

"OK, then let's hang out this evening."

"OK. Take it easy on the young dudes on court!"

"Hell nah, I am going to try to wipe all their young asses. If you come with me, we could teach these young dudes a lesson. Are you sure you don't want to come?"

"Nah, I need a break from ball. Come get me when you are done."

Chapter 12

The last week in Chicago, I just spent time with family members and some of the locals in K-Town.

My grandfather and I didn't seem to have the same connection. In his eyes I was now a man capable of making my own decisions. We would talk, but he just wanted to know how college was going. He didn't have any suggestions or input. It was the first time I'd felt distance between us.

One night I was upstairs talking to Aunt Betty and my grandfather came up. We all sat around the table talking and having fun. We talked about my first year in college and what I had learned being on my own. He looked proud, but then the conversation changed drastically.

My grandfather asked me to go next door with him to visit our neighbors, a mother and three daughters. I thought his request was strange, especially since it was made in front of Aunt Betty and several of her kids. He asked several more times. I kept politely declining. I guess he got it. I was not going next door with him. Once he left and went back downstairs I asked Aunt Betty, "Why is Daddy trying to get me to go to our neighbors' house with him?"

"Daddy wanted you to go with him so he could see the neighbors."

"I don't have a connection with our neighbors. Why does he want to see them?"

She hesitated for a moment. It was hard for her to say that Daddy had started having affairs with other women in the community.

"He has one lady he sees regularly. She lives down the street."

Aunt Ida later confirmed this.

That second old elephant in the living room finally had a name: *Infidelity*.

My grandfather knew that I was studying hard for all my classes. He knew his work ethic was deeply planted within me. If I failed academically, it would be unacceptable, and I would get a swift visit from Aunt Ida.

So how in the world did he reconcile lying and cheating on his wife? Didn't he give a damn about how that looked to me? I couldn't believe it.

Was his request that I visit our neighbors with him some kind of manhood test? Did he want me to collude in his betrayal? Didn't he realize the message he was sending me and the other kids about how he felt about women?

When Daddy passed away in 1992, Aunt Ida pointed out one of his women friends at his funeral. I wondered how long they'd had a relationship. Perhaps this was one of the reasons for my grandmother's unhappiness. Did she know of his infidelities?

Like former presidents of our country, CEOs of corporations, professional athletes, musicians, and some everyday hard-working men, my grandfather was a man with his own particular demons when it came to women. Whether or not he called them demons or believed they had a valid place in his code of living, I will never know.

When, as a young man, I made this disturbing discovery about my grandfather, I knew this behavior would not be in *my* value system, even though the grandfather I still loved clearly thought it was acceptable behavior. And if he failed to abide by aspects of *his* code, did it mean that one day, in some manner, I would be tempted to fail in some of mine as well? That thought scares me to death.

I was learning that no matter how polished we might look on the outside, human beings are not perfect. And that included my grandfather.

When Daddy passed away, I wondered, *Am I now the patriarch of the family? What does it mean to be a patriarch?* I tried to understand how he had justified betrayal to his wife, how he could look her in the eye. But could I understand?

What are we seeking when we have a sexual relationship with someone other than our spouse? Affairs often make great conversation topics among our male friends. So are we using affairs to try to validate our manhood?

Are affairs simply an addiction, as some claim?

What makes some of us pursue these attractions for other women while others among us allow them to dissipate as fleeting thoughts?

At that time of my life, I only had questions, no answers. To be truthful, I still have them.

Chapter 13

June 1976. I was back at St. Thomas, where I attended summer school and found work. Coach Feely recommended that I stay away from basketball for the summer. Why not try tennis? he asked. I looked at him with a young man's arrogant smirk.

"Coach, you want me to play tennis?"

"Yeah, why don't you give it a try?"

"Why would you want me to play tennis? That's an easy game, Coach."

Coach laughed. "Billy, tennis is not an easy sport."

His voice had a raspy tone. Whenever he spoke, his hands often fluttered absentmindedly across his chest and shoulders. The movement was eccentric, comical. Some of the basketball players would imitate and mock his peculiar movements (you know how kids see great humor in our physical peculiarities), but only when he was not watching.

"Uhhhhhh, Coach, yes it is." I wanted to be respectful, but I could feel another smirk curling my lips.

"OK, tomorrow let's play and I'll show you that it's not easy."

"OK, I will get back to the dorm after work around 5 p.m."

That following evening, I realized I did not even have a tennis racket. So I asked a few summer school students if I could borrow one.

I got dressed in my basketball shorts and basketball shoes. Sporting a Dunlap wooden tennis racket with broken strings, I set out, ready to teach my coach a lesson.

We arrived at the courts behind Ireland Hall. He noticed my attire.

"Billy, the first lesson I will give you is how to dress for tennis," he said. "Do you have any tennis shorts? Basketball shorts are not proper tennis attire. You need tennis shoes, not basketball shoes. What do you think we are playing, a pickup basketball game?"

"Ah, Coach, this won't take long. Let's play."

Again, he looked at me with that admonishing "you silly young man" look. Then he taught me the scoring system and the rules of the game. I was getting restless. I just wanted to give him a lesson and be done with it.

I soon realized that I was the only one running and chasing the tennis balls.

"What's the score, Coach?"

"Three games for me and zero for you. Easy game, huh, Billy?"

He finished me off very easily, with the first set at 6–0. We met at the net.

"Billy, tennis is a great game, right? You can play when you are my age and older. You can play with your kids, family, spouse, and friends for many years. It's a gentleman's sport where rules are to be respected and honored. It's an easy game, huh, Billy?"

We smiled at one another. Thoughts rushed into my mind of our time at the Twins game in June when I told him I was attending St. Thomas even if the other coaches called. Simultaneously, I felt a flood of emotions about my grandfather and the lessons I'd learned from him at baseball games.

Manhood lessons started with my grandfather. Now the

lessons had another source, another venue. Coach Tom Feely had just humbled me. He was in his late 50s, I was twenty, and I was the one gasping for air.

The next set score was the same—6–0 for Coach Feely.

Tennis and humility! That day, arrogance was drained out of me by a fifty–plus-year-old man. Thanks, Coach Feely.

And that day, I fell in love with tennis. It marked an important moment that would eventually lead to my life's work.

In 1977, my new love for tennis led to my meeting a new priest who lived in the dorms during the summer. The tennis courts were available to all the students, faculty, staff, and local residents. After work in the summer I would rush back to the dorms and race down to the tennis courts. The varsity tennis players were acting as teaching pros and taking reservations during the summer. We all played tennis quite a bit during the summer. This new priest was also frequently on the courts in the evenings.

One evening we finally introduced ourselves. His name was Father Dennis Dease. I later took one of his theology classes, and we remain great friends to this day. As I write, Father Dease is president of the University of St. Thomas.

Melvin "Heavy" Freeman and I spent many nights in our dorm rooms talking about life. On weekends, we went fishing with Coach Vaughn or socialized with students from nearby Macalester College.

Heavy also spent many weekends with Sharon. I knew she was special in his life and noticed how that relationship settled him. Sharon's father, who we just called Mr. Zachary, came to some of our basketball games. He'd loudly cheer for us from the stands, and everyone in the building could hear him. He reminded me of Coach Vaughn, a strong presence commanding respect. Mr. Zachary was very knowledgeable about life and sports, and a great father figure for both Heavy and me. He demonstrated a strict and stern family value system. The world could use a few more Mr. Zacharys. I was truly happy for Heavy, because I knew he was very much in love with Sharon. Heavy and Sharon were married in 1979 and later had two wonderful sons, Melvin Jr. and Marcus.

These events nurtured us through my four years at St. Thomas. What I cherish most about those years were the relationships I established. My family values helped me connect with many people I consider friends to this day. Thanks to my experience at St. Thomas, searching outside my family for similar values was getting a little easier.

My biological father, Larry, and I maintained a wonderful, authentic relationship throughout my four years at St. Thomas. We had many conversations over the phone. If I needed any help, he was always willing to oblige.

1979. My senior year at St. Thomas. I contacted Aunt Betty about my graduation date, and she informed Aunt Ida, Aunt Sam, and my mother, Irene. They all attended. It was a wonderful experience having them all there. I deeply felt all of their support, pride, and love.

All of my aunts felt proud of me on graduation day. I had accomplished a cherished family value—higher education. And I would soon be bound for a banking industry job in Phoenix, Arizona.

Now what? I wondered:

Are my aunts wondering what my life would be like in the real world? I know I am.

Is this the end of my education? Will there be more? If so, what will it consist of?

Will I get married and have children? What type of husband and father will I be?

Will I like Phoenix? What if I don't like the job and the area?

Chapter 14

I moved to Phoenix in June 1979. But I just did not like Phoenix. It never felt like a community. So many people from different parts of our country migrate there and seemed to me to be pretending to be more than what they really were.

Andre "Champ" Wakefield from Crane High was trying out for the Phoenix Suns professional basketball team. Champ and I met on several occasions. It was good to see Champ and reconnect with him.

I was in constant contact with Heavy while l lived in Phoenix.

But my experience in Phoenix lasted only one year. Soon I was Minnesota bound again.

April 1980. I arrived back in St. Paul. Heavy and Sharon invited me to stay with them for a few months until I found employment with the Control Data Corporation and saved up enough money to move into my own apartment. Control Data had a world distribution center located just blocks from Heavy and Sharon's home. I was a buyer there. During those few months at Heavy's home, we constantly talked about our lives and what we wanted to accomplish.

Larry and I shared only a few conversations that year I lived and worked in Phoenix, but I spoke to him quite often after I'd returned to St. Paul, resettled, and found employment.

I played lots of tennis after work and met several local players. There were two courts at the Martin Luther King Center where most of the African-American tennis players gathered. They accepted me into their little tennis community.

One evening in late May, after we finished on the tennis courts, my friend George Breckenridge asked me if I wanted to get a bite to eat. We went to Sweeney's Bar and Grill.

Entering the establishment with George, I spotted two beautiful African-American women at a table talking. I was totally focused on them.

"George, those are two of the most beautiful women I have ever seen."

"Where?"

I didn't want to be crass by pointing! "Over there by the window."

"Oh, I know them; they're my friends Gail and Margo. Do you want to meet them?"

"Yeah."

Before I could utter another word, we were at their table. George was not the shy type; he readily approached their table and introduced me to Gail and Margo.

I was immediately attracted to Gail Lamb. She had a special glow about her. We four ended up talking well into the evening.

Gail made it very clear that romance was out of the question. She told me that her divorce had been finalized just a couple of months before and that she had no interest in moving quickly into another relationship. I had to choose being her friend and give up on the possibility that a romantic relationship would ever happen. I chose to honor her request, and we became the best of friends.

Gail had a zest for learning and growing. She was inspiring to be around. She questioned her surroundings. She loved reading. We both were on an introspective journey, both looking for answers about our lives.

How would I handle my romantic attraction to Gail Lamb? She wanted to be "friends." How could I explain my "friendship" with a beautiful lady to my male friends? Of course I didn't even try to explain.

Throughout our eight-year friendship, I learned to set romantic and sexual feelings aside. I was forced to learn how to develop an authentic, loving, caring, *platonic* relationship with a woman. During those eight years I connected deeply with Gail. Now, I won't say I was happy about the lack of a romance, about being just friends. But I sure did learn patience!

I remember clearly the first time I met Gail's dad, Fulton Lamb. He had a lean, athletic build; he looked like an Olympic pole vaulter and had a piercing look, much like my grandfather's. He was born in Arkansas and migrated to Minnesota in the late 1940s with his wife, Helen.

Gail and I were friends, living next door to one another in St. Paul, when I first met Fulton. The look he gave me upon our meeting was suspicious and intense—it could have bored a hole through my heart. Several years later, when Gail and I lived as roommates in south Minneapolis, Gail told me her father was livid because he thought I was dishonoring his daughter. Why were we living together and not married? Gail assured him that we were good friends, sharing expenses, and were not romantically involved.

Fulton roared, "Baby girl, can't no man live with a woman he likes and not have sex with her. Who do y'all think you foolin'?"

While he never called me this to my face, Gail told me her dad used to call me "the weasel." Apparently, weasels are secretive, evasive, and untrustworthy.

I admit I admired his protective attitude when it came to his only daughter. His manhood and fatherhood led him to want to protect her. I knew if I were in his shoes I probably would have reacted the same way. During the many visits to Gail's parents' home, I discovered Fulton was a brilliant and wise man, like my grandfather.

In the early 1940s, Fulton had enrolled with the Tuskegee Airmen in Alabama, a program in which African-American men were trained to become pilots. He had the mind of an engineer and could repair anything electrical or mechanical. He also loved baseball; the Minnesota Twins were his favorite team. He loved Harmon Killebrew and Rod Carew.

I also met her older brothers, Lynn and John Michael. John Michael played basketball at Arizona State University and professionally in Belgium. He was 6 feet 10, very articulate and worldly, and loved reading. He and I were similar in many ways. We both felt comfortable being alone and loved our independence, were self-reliant, and did not want anyone helping us. We had our fathers' work ethic. We both eventually became entrepreneurs and great friends, and now communicate regularly. When I take golfing trips to Arizona to get away from the cold Minnesota winters, I stay with John Michael. The topics we talk about!

Gail's mother, Helen Lamb, was an angel—the third one I have met in my life. She had a welcoming, loving smile with warmth that removed all of the tension between Gail and her dad. We spent many holidays in St. Paul with Fulton and Helen.

My only regret is that Mr. Lamb passed away several years before Gail and I got married in 1990.

To Mr. Fulton Lamb: The family value system instilled in me produced an introspective journey that prepared me to meet your wonderful daughter, Gail. If you were alive today, you would be proud of the man I have become. You would be proud of how I respect, honor, cherish, and love your only daughter. Oh, how I wish we could talk now; perhaps we would talk about the Twins, and laugh like my grandfather and I did at the White Sox games in Chicago. I hope you would be proud of me and the work your daughter and I are doing.

The more I continued to learn about myself, the unhappier I became working in the corporate world. I felt like something was missing in my life. I decided that corporate work was not for me. I signed with temp agencies, did some freelancing, and got more work than I could handle.

As I thought back on my life and my family values, I knew that my aunts were in my life for many reasons, and one of them was to prepare me to meet Gail Lamb. From my aunts I had learned to be totally comfortable in the presence of women. With Gail I experienced being with a woman I loved, but I had to respect her boundaries.

Heavy and I stayed in touch while he lived in St. Paul and I lived in south Minneapolis. One day in the mid-1980s, our conversation focused on sad news. Coach Vaughn had been killed in a car accident in Arkansas. Heavy and I talked for a long while about Coach Vaughn, and I shed many tears that sad day over his passing.

After eight years of being my best friend, Gail moved to Nevada. Soon after, Ron Predovich, a co-worker at my long-term assignment, talked Ron Grass and me into playing in a basketball league with him in Eden Prairie, a western suburb of Minneapolis. My car was not the most reliable, so I was late for a few games because of car problems.

Ron suggested I just move to Eden Prairie. He would tease me by saying, "Yeah, William, I can see you moving out to Eden Prairie, getting married, having some children, and driving around in a mini van to sporting events on the weekend. What would your homeboys back in Chicago think of you then?" Of course I thought he was nuts, but we did have many laughs. But after giving it some thought, I realized it made sense to move to Eden Prairie to be closer to work.

My freelance assignment happened to be in Eden Prairie. It was a long-term assignment that eventually turned into a full-time position. Ron Grass was happy. No more being late for basketball games.

I met many new friends at a local fitness club I frequented several times a week after work. They encouraged me to get back into the corporate world. Most of them thought I was destroying my career by doing freelance work; they wondered why I would want to freelance despite my intelligence and work experience. A few did understand the importance of how I was living and what I was doing.

I knew my new friends would not understand the internal work I was doing. They only saw the outside. But the real work was going on inside of me.

I was actually working harder than I ever had in any job, but it was internally directed. I had nothing to show for what I was accomplishing, at least in the eyes of others.

In our culture, if we work hard, we are rewarded with accolades, plaques on the wall, money in the bank, things we can show and tell. I had none of those things. I did not have a fancy house, an expensive car, a promising career. I had no kids to shuttle around on weekends to sporting activities, and no beautiful girlfriend or wife. But I was happy with my life. I accepted my friends' advice as well-meaning, but I knew there was something else I was preparing for. I just didn't know what it was.

I often was the one some of the guys would confide in. Some would share with me their concerns about working so much and not really being happy with their work but seeing no alternatives, and the stress of being the provider, of spending their weekends taking their kids to so many sporting events. Some said they felt trapped.

I would wonder, why do they confide in me? I did not represent success in the conventional sense. Did they sense that I was happy without having any externals to show for it?

During those years, it was friends like Tom and Dan Boulay, Decker Velie, Tom and Mary Quiring, Linda LeClaire, Pam Welter, Ron Predovich, and Ron Grass who truly understood.

Fall 1981. I'd just arrived home to my apartment that evening. The phone rang.

"Hi, Lil Henry, this is your cousin John Albert calling from Harvey. You know that Butch and I were very close and we spent lots of time together."

"Yes, I know," I said.

"Well, I got some very bad news." He paused. "I'm sorry to say that Butch just passed away."

Oh, man, *nooo. Noooo.* "When did he die?"

"Last week. I hope you will be able to make his funeral."

I was stunned, speechless, and deeply saddened.

Larry Woodson was only forty-three years old. A heart attack took him from me just six years after we'd met.

Almost thirty years later, not a day passes without me thinking of Larry Woodson, my father. What would he say to me, about the life I've created for myself? I'd like to think I know what his response would be—the same as my grandfather's remark on our front porch thirty-five years ago: *"I'm proud of you. I love you."*

Chapter **15**

D ecember 1989. Gail, who was still living in Nevada, and I got back in contact with one another after a hiatus of about eighteen months. She had been a constant companion for almost ten years. It was great talking to her again.

One evening in January 1990, our conversation seemed different. We continued to update one another on our lives. Then, out of the blue, she asked if we should get married. She said she was ready. I was shocked but said yes instantly. I was not in a relationship at the time and I had started to want a serious relationship with someone. My life as a single guy consisted of working, playing tennis every day, and playing in basketball leagues with Ron Grass.

Gail moved back to Minnesota, and we were married on April 13, 1990. One of my friends from work, Tom Quiring, his wife, Mary, their four-year-old son, Keith, their newborn son, John, and their springer spaniel, Kirby, stood up for us. Thanks, Tom "Q-Dude" and Mary, for your loving support during a memorable time in my life.

I remember the looks and comments from my friends at the

health club. One was Decker Velie, who I had met through tennis. We played tennis together often and had wonderful talks afterward.

"Decker, I am getting married."

"What do you mean you are getting married? You don't even have a girlfriend!"

"I know; she is a wonderful friend of ten years."

"Man, that's a quick decision. Don't you want to just get engaged first?"

"No, there is no need for being engaged. She is the one for me. I was in love with her the first day we met almost ten years ago. Back then she just wanted to be friends and neither one of us was ready for a serious relationship. Now she is in love with me!"

"Man, I can't wait to meet her! She must be something special, because you are very excited. How about Bonnie and I host a wedding party for you in May or June?"

"Thanks, Decker, that's very nice that you want to do this for us."

After we got married in April, Decker and Bonnie Velie and Dave and Linda Nash helped arrange a wedding party at the Velie home. All of my friends from the tennis community attended. We had a wonderful time.

A few months after we were married, Gail and I talked about me having more meaningful employment. The conversation never centered on reentering the corporate world. I shared with Gail what I learned about myself, about my introspective years working in Eden Prairie, and my current feelings of discontent.

"You seem to really enjoy playing tennis."

"Yes, I do; I really enjoy it."

She turned around. Her eyes met mine with warmth and compassion. "Why don't you try to get a job working in the tennis industry? You would be great working with kids and adults."

"That's a great idea. I will start contacting some of my tennis friends."

Several weeks later I committed to becoming a professional

tennis instructor. I took a series of certification tests and volunteered teaching tennis to gain experience.

Later in 1990, Jerry Noyce hired me as a professional tennis instructor. He was the director of tennis at the Northwest Racquet Club. What I liked about working for Jerry was his hands-off approach. He trusted you to be responsible yet motivated to develop your own client base. He was the perfect boss for me because I needed no handholding. I had my grandparents' work ethic.

I taught tennis for five years and loved every minute of it. It set the stage for me to find my life's purpose. During my five years of working for Jerry as a professional tennis instructor, I found that I was able to easily bond with and gain the trust of young people. They wanted me to meet their parents. Some took private lessons from me just to talk. I found myself teaching entire families.

Chapter 16

After five years of teaching, I knew I wanted to continue helping people. I truly enjoyed teaching and bonding with the young people, with the women on my teams in the daytime league, and their families.

Yet I still felt there was more that I needed to be doing and contributing. I had no clue what it was during those years. Teaching tennis gave me direct contact with the customer. If they didn't like you, they wouldn't come back. You got instant feedback, and the women were direct and honest. I cherish their honesty and friendship to this day.

Later that year I learned through friends that the U.S. Tennis Association had created a new part-time position called multicultural tennis director. It was created to generate more interest from and develop tennis programs in communities of color and schools.

I interviewed with Marcia Bach, executive director of the Northern Section of the United States Tennis Association, and Wendell Willis, chairman of the Multicultural Council, and was offered the job. I stayed on as a professional tennis instructor part time, but after a few months moved into my new position with the USTA full time.

One of my friends and professional colleagues, Mike Ach, mentioned he had a friend I should meet, Fred Wells. He said Fred was a very understanding and caring person who loved helping young people. Fred and I eventually met, and he made contributions to the USTA that allowed me to come aboard full time. Fred's support and friendship helped set in motion my realization of my life's purpose.

Two situations stood out with me as the new and first multicultural tennis director. The first presented itself when several African-American parents wanted me to get their kids into an advanced program called the Area Training Center for highly rated junior tennis players. Teaching professionals who were friends of mine taught in the Area Training Center program.

The parents and volunteers said, "Bill, you need to try and get some of our advanced kids in the Area Training Centers so they can train and compete with the ranked players."

To this day, I am not sure if it was me or my grandfather speaking.

"No, we are not going to do that. Why should we beg and plead to get our kids into a program they don't qualify for? If we want a special training program for our advanced kids, then let's create our own program."

Silence. Angry, confused looks. I stood my ground so that they could think about what I just said. I was the youngest person in the room. All of the others were parents or grandparents of some of the players, great local players themselves or volunteers dedicated to helping young people of color.

"Bill, so what are you suggesting we do?" They seemed bewildered. "We need to get our kids on an equal playing field with the rest of the juniors in our section."

"Let's create our own training center and call it the Urban Training Center. I know all of the tennis professionals who run the

USTA Area Training Center Program. They are my friends, and they would be happy to help us. When we get our own training center established, I will invite several to come as guest instructors. Several of us here are certified professional tennis instructors. We should establish our own event. As part of my responsibilities as the multicultural tennis director, I will get the funding to take care of the court time and expenses for the event. This is something we can readily do for ourselves."

"When do you think we should have the first event?"

"You all decide on how often you want to have the training centers. I would suggest once a quarter, but let me know and I will take care of the rest."

As I left the meeting that evening, most of them remained talking among themselves and wondering what had just happened. I did notice that they were excited.

We eventually established weekend programs as well. We had a Saturday morning program that was open to *all* kids, whether they were advanced, intermediate, or beginners, and their parents participated as well.

The second situation presented itself the evening I met Henrietta Falconer. Her son, Eric, was one of the advanced players in our program. She thanked me for arranging all the programs for the youth.

"Bill, the kids are really enjoying the programs you've established," she said. "Eric loves coming to the tennis programs. He loves the fact that you take time to work out with him personally. He really admires you.

"Thanks, Henrietta. Eric is a fine young man."

"Bill, have you ever heard of the Hennepin County Home School?"

"No, I haven't," I replied.

"It's an adolescent treatment facility run by Hennepin county. The kids there could really benefit from having you in their lives and a tennis program like this. I see the positive impact on Eric. All the young men there are on probation. Most of them don't know their fathers or have any positive role models in their lives. If you are interested in establishing a tennis program for them, I know a lady there you could contact."

"Henrietta, if you think they would benefit, I will follow up."

Henrietta gave me the contacts at the Hennepin County Home School.

Its administrators told me its history. It was a residential treatment facility for adolescents. Hennepin County has a collaborative relationship with the Hopkins School District to run the high school education component of the program. The tennis program would be under the school's jurisdiction. Hennepin County administrators agreed to give the tennis program a try.

Chapter 17

Youth, youth, and more youth, clamoring for my attention. That first year at the Hennepin County Home School was overwhelming, eye-opening, fulfilling.

"Mr. Roddy, will we see you again next Monday? Mr. Roddy, are you coming to our cottage on Saturday for visitation? Would you mind hanging out with me for a few minutes when you come?"

These were typical requests most Mondays. But this Monday was different. For the last six months I had recruited Gail to visit with the young people in the cottages on weekends. We visited as a couple and cooked meals with them. The youth seemed to love to see us come out together and spend time with them.

Several weeks had passed since my conversation with Principal Mary Slinde and the feeling of knowing my life's purpose. I had never shared my conversation or thoughts with anyone, including Gail.

On my way home from work at the USTA one evening, flashes of my grandfather's values came pouring out to me. It was as if he were with me, standing over me, saying, *Remain independent. Make your own decisions. Never ask anyone to do something for you that you can do for yourself.* I stopped at the library before I drove home that evening. When I got home, Gail was in the kitchen preparing dinner. I asked her if I could talk to her for a few minutes before we ate.

"Baby, you know I love working with the youth at the Hennepin County Home School and enjoy you accompanying me on the weekends in the cottages."

"I know you love it, because I can see how effective you are with the young men."

"How about I quit my position at the USTA and we start a business together that works with the youth full time?" I nervously awaited her reply. Would she think I'd lost my mind to make such a suggestion?

"Hmmm. OK. But just one thing—do we know anything about how to start a business?"

"I thought you might ask that question. I stopped at the library and picked up these four books."

"What are they?"

"Books on starting and running companies. All about understanding the different business structures like LLCs, nonprofits, S-Corporations, and C-Corporations."

"OK, let's read them and then decide where to go from there."

Within two weeks we had read all four books and decided on a nonprofit structure. We were on our way to starting a business from the ground floor up.

After three years of working for Marcia Bach, executive director of the U.S. Tennis Association, I knew I could not work for anyone else. She was the perfect boss for me. She had total confidence in her staff. She had the forgiveness and patience of Aunt Sam and the wisdom and guidance of Aunt Betty. She had spoiled me to the core. Working for anyone else would have been extremely disappointing.

My biggest emotional obstacle was informing Marcia that I was leaving. I knew that she would understand, but that it would also be an emotional ordeal for both of us. Marcia truly cared for the well-being of her staff.

I remember the day I left my resignation letter on Marcia's desk. When she arrived, on her way to her office, Marcia always made sure she spoke to the staff members who were in the office that day. That day I noticed she was a little stressed as she sat down in her chair. I noticed her reading other notes, looking at phone messages she needed to return and generally getting situated for the day. Then I noticed she was very still for a while. I had placed my resignation letter right on her chair so that no other letters, memos, or phone messages could cover it.

After a few minutes she rose from her desk and left the office for several hours. I knew she had read my resignation letter. At that moment I felt absolutely awful. But I knew that once I had the opportunity to explain to her why I was leaving, she would be supportive and understanding.

Over the next few days, Gail and I filled out IRS determination letter applications, incorporated the business, and set up meetings with the Hennepin County Home School superintendent and her managers to get their support for our new business venture.

We arranged to meet with a group of young people at the home school to get their support and feedback. These youths helped us develop all our current services.

Two days after I'd delivered my resignation letter, Marcia called me into her office. I knew this would be a very emotional and difficult meeting due to our mutual respect for one another. I was leaving an industry and position I loved. Most of my friends who were teaching and working in the tennis industry were at a loss as to why I was leaving. How could I leave such a wonderful position to venture off into the unknown? They didn't know about the value system instilled in me in childhood. They only had witnessed the lifelong friendships that were established as a result.

"Bill, I read your resignation letter a few days ago," Marcia said. "I had lots of other things on my mind that week. When I read your letter, I had to leave the office for the day. I was not in a position to talk to you. I am sorry for the delay, but I know you have thought about this and did not come to this conclusion hastily. Is there anything I can do to make you stay? If not, what can I do to support you?"

At that moment Marcia appeared to me as Aunt Sam. She had the same supportive and unconditionally loving eyes and presence.

"Marcia, you have been wonderful to work for these last years," I said. "When I go to the Hennepin County Home School and spend time with youth who migrated to Minnesota from Chicago, Gary, and Detroit for a better life, I realize they can't even read and have no father figures in their lives. I must be totally honest. How is tennis going to help them read?"

"How can I continue to promote tennis, which is another sport? Young African-American men are already obsessed with sports, especially basketball and football. I don't want to create another obsession. I want to be an ambassador for the values my grandparents, aunts, and other adult mentors in our community who cared about young people taught me while I was growing up in Chicago. I feel this is missing in our community, our state, and our country. We as a country have lost those values."

Silence fell, and then she spoke.

"I totally understand, Bill. Who would you recommend to take your place?"

I knew then that Marcia understood my decision and acknowledged my life's purpose was calling. She supported me and wished me well on my new venture. Marcia and I remain friends to this day.

I thought about it for a while and recommended Tony Stingley for the job I was leaving. Tony was one of the volunteers I had recruited. He had good administrative skills, loved the game of tennis, and had his own kids in our tennis program.

He was a great father and husband, and I knew he could take over and catapult the program to higher levels. And in fact, he is still doing an outstanding job at the USTA.

My destiny was calling me elsewhere.

Epilogue

July 1997. We founded Osiris Organization with great hopes for the future of our youth and our country.

Several of the young men I became close to had literacy issues, no fathers or grandparents, no loving aunts, no Finks, no Ernest Leaks, no Heavys, no Mr. Zacharys, no Coach Vaughns, no Coach Whites in their young lives, no employment waiting for them, and no one waiting to help them in their communities once they left the Hennepin County Home School.

We started our organization to share, teach, demonstrate, and incorporate a value system that prizes education, reading, respecting our elders, grandparents, mothers, fathers, aunts, and teachers, and valuing the things that have made our nation great, including entrepreneurship.

So now you see: My grandfather's values inspired me to work with youth full time. I knew I had to leave the tennis industry to do so. These young people at the Hennepin County Home School needed to see me in a role that focused more on education and building life skills.

They needed me to pass on to them what my grandfather so lovingly gave me: a set of values that would prepare me for manhood.

Gail and I and our staff witness firsthand the neglect of family values that has caused so much unnecessary pain in the lives of so many. This neglect puts an enormous burden on our communities and our nation.

As I've written this book and reflected on the value system I witnessed growing up in Chicago during the 1960s and '70s, I've pondered a great deal.

We witnessed our parents getting us up early in the morning, preparing themselves to go to work while getting us ready to go to school. Multiple family members often lived together. Everyone shared in the responsibility of nurturing the children in the family and community.

Our baseball field on the corner of 13th Street and Leavitt Avenue wasn't the most immaculately groomed. There was no scoreboard, no night-lights, no dugout to rest our young legs between innings, but we didn't know any different. Our team was called "Sluggers." Our uniform consisted of the official baseball shirt with the name on it, but we wore our blue jeans to complete the uniform. Who knows what happened to the uniform pants? We had no baseball cleats.

Our jerseys were cream-colored, with dark-blue pin stripes; "Sluggers" was embroidered in crimson with dark-blue bordering around each letter. Some of the jerseys fit perfectly, some were baggy on our little bodies and ended just above our young knees. The jerseys were passed down to us, and we wore them proudly.

We all bonded through baseball on this field and had fun coming together as a community, adults and kids alike.

Brainard, our elementary school, was where I met most of my friends, who then accompanied me through junior and senior high schools. There was so much more lifestyle stability—parents kept the same job for thirty or forty years, so kids spent their entire formative years together.

The streets of our community were filled with homes, small apartment buildings, a few factories and taverns, mom-and-pop restaurants and candy stores, shoe repair shops, butcher shops, furniture stores, a community center where we learned to play ping-pong and shoot pool. After school we always walked home, chattering about kid stuff.

We passed Ms. Mary's restaurant, captivated by the aroma of the delicious soul food she was preparing for her dinner customers— collard greens, chicken, pork chops, pies, and other tasty dishes. We passed adults sitting on their front porches; they would wave to us and ask us how school had gone that day. We passed Ben's Shoe Shop, located in his basement, where he was always hard at work. At one point or another most of us worked for Ben, shining shoes in his shop. We passed Mickey's corner grocery and candy store, and the sugary aroma consumed us, begging us to come right on in!

We passed the Acme Barrel Company and heard and saw the barrels rolling over the assembly lines. We watched the workers, men in knee-high black rubber boots, handling the barrels, sweat dripping down their faces, necks, and chests. Some of the men stood outside on their breaks, drinking sodas and smoking cigarettes. As we passed by they would call out to us, "Y'all make sure y'all stay in school and do good, y'all hear? Y'all don't want to be working in this factory like us when you grow up."

We passed two taverns, TopHat's and Rockbottom, and could hear the music of James Brown or Aretha Franklin blasting out.

Weekends, the young adults would race their cars along Hastings Street. It was pure entertainment. During the week, after work, the young drag racers would arrive home and toil out in the alleys and streets, prepping their cars for the weekend races. The crowds were enormous as we gathered on either side of Hastings to watch the races. During the week, baseball was king. But on the late evening on the weekends, racing *ruled!*

Roosevelt Road, Western Avenue, 13th Street, Leavitt, Claremont, Heath, Washburn, Damen, Oakley, Hoyne, Ashland, and

Hastings. These streets are burned in my memory as the landmarks of my village, and these were the years I learned my values. We had our issues, like any community. Still, it *was our village.*

We hope that by setting in motion a self-reliant consciousness and an entrepreneurial spirit in our young people, we can perhaps lay a framework that could help get us back on track.

I feel proud as an American to try. I wonder what my grandfather would say?

Let's imagine for a moment that he were still alive.

"Daddy, how would you get our great nation back on track?"

"Son, I don't have all of your education and business experience. Here are my brief thoughts, and please forgive me if I offend anyone.

"All I see now is a country buying shit you don't need just to keep the economy afloat. Son, what has happened to the country? How long can the average working-class family afford to continue buying shit they don't need? Son, how many pair of blue jeans does it take to satisfy a young person nowadays?"

"Daddy, please remember the language. People might find it offensive."

"OK, son, I see your point. I got a whole lot more to say, but not enough time. I know this is your first book, and I don't want to get in the way."

"Daddy, you are not getting in the way, but we will address your other thoughts at a later time."

"Son, this is why I wanted you to learn to read and eventually become an entrepreneur. I wanted you to be independent, to not let anyone tell you what to believe or what to think. I learned so much from running the farm in Arkansas. I hoped you would look at life through your own eyes and not someone else's, be able to live your life to the fullest and not be concerned about what others think of you, and not look for someone to take care of you. Please let me finish these last thoughts before I leave.

"Son, remember our talks at the White Sox games when you were young?"

"Not all of them," I would say to him. "You shared so much information with me. Daddy, we don't have enough time for all of your thoughts. Would you be available in a few years if there were more interest in your thoughts?"

"Hell, yeah. I would be happy to share more of my thoughts in great detail. *How 'bout those White Sox in the 2005 World Series? They finally listened to me. Stay in touch with me, son.*"

Through my years as an entrepreneur, I have come to realize that we are still a gracious nation. Americans are the first to help another nation in need. We volunteer. We donate money to worthy causes. Any citizen of our country can start his or her own business. We are free to choose what faith to follow, or to follow none at all. We are a nation of creators, inventors, and innovators. We have opportunities to accomplish marvelous things. We have the freedom to accomplish anything our hearts desire. Given these truths and opportunities, can you see why we stress entrepreneurial development to the young people we serve?

I wish all those who have read this book much love. Thanks for your patience and understanding. I hope that by sharing some of my memories about how I developed my values, I also have encouraged you to think about and reflect on your own values. Perhaps you have a book inside of you to write and share? I would love to read it.

I have to go now. Young entrepreneurs are waiting for us.

"Hey, Mr. Roddy, how are those new laws going to affect my business? Are we going to pursue the joint-venture business opportunities we discussed at our last monthly business collaboration meeting?

"Man, Mr. Roddy, if this works out, I will need to bring on some help! Job creation—isn't that what we as entrepreneurs do for our country?

"Glad we all got each other's back, Mr. Roddy!"

Wonderful words from one of our young, passionate, and patriotic entrepreneurs.

Acknowledgements

To all of those who supported me through the past and into the present,

Ed and Martha Gshneidner, Laurie and Jan Reardon, Jack and Rhonda Liebo, Bruce and Julia Wiessner, Dr. Bryce Young, Paul and Janet Tolzmann, Zvi Frankfurt, Josh LeClaire, Dennis McGrath, Betsy Buckley, JoAnne Pastel, Ernie Greene, Babatunde Abe, Lolita Edward Johns, Coach Steve Fritz, Dr. Fairchild, Coach Flood, Coach Dwayne Dietz and family, James Willis, Terrence J. Fleming, Esq., James F. Morrison, Esq., Greg Hendricks, Tom E. Lynn "the ultimate rebounder," Steve Karel, Calvin and Darnell Johnson, while living in our village along with my grandparents and family, taught me how to throw a curve ball, Michael Peterson, Edward "Bobo" Williams, Mark "Butterball" Garrett, Marvin Nelson, much love to my friends who lived in the Rockwell, Henry Horner, and The Village Public Housing Projects while attending Crane High School with me in the 70', Mr. Bonner, Mr. Armstrong, Ms Daniels, Ronald L. and Linda

Burrell, Dr. Remi Douah, Corky and Juli Wiseman, Keith Kelly,
Henry Sharpe III, Elberta Butler, Laurie Kuepker, Jason Dufloth,
Duane Nelson Jr., Michael Butler Jr., Vann and Phetmany Ek,
Cortez, Cordell and Cameron Wilson, Boun Vilailath, Mr. and
Mrs. Lincoln Jones, Larry Wilson, Michael Patterson, Harvey
Humes, Morgan Smith, Ms. Loving, Connie Woodson, Ron
Predovich, Monte and Nicole Moisman, Darzel Price, Pauline
Vivian Dantzler, Bertha "Kitty" Young, Bob Sansevere, Pamela
Miller, the world's greatest editor, Pat Colbert, Margaret Spiegel,
Chris White, Jeff Antonson, Kurt Vegdahl, Michele Russell, Paul
Kelley, Brad Barclay, Amy Wener, Bob Kershaw, Rachel Aiken,
John and Linda Stoddart, Tom Stoddart, Brian Jones, Dr. Tom
Sutton, Roland Green, Larry Weatherspoon, Robert Ramphal,
Gordon Reid, Alvin Hines, Dave McCarthy, Brace Helgeson,
Adam and Alita LaBrie, Ann Malling, Anne and Harlan Sween,
Steve and Arlene Kessel, Kim Upsher, Fred Budde, Ken Cychosz,
Ray Costello, Tim Jochim, Terry Wise, Tom Bezik, Gregory
Bingham, Glenda Jackson, Greg Jackson, Pat Simerson-Wallred,
Mark DePauw, Sue Sinna, Duane Perry, Rolando Jackson, Kiley
Demery, Rodney Smith, Ken Jones, Quentin and Sally Hietpas,
Ernest Draper, Jeff Schissler, Jim and Leslie Skyrms, Ms. Spikes,
Ms. Douglas, Rodger Swanson, Brad Swanson, Larry Henry,
Larry Smith, Keith "Keke" Williams, Sandy Martin and family,
Jan Schissel, Rich "Dick" Mammen, Carole Anderson, Mark and
Cindy Webber, Jack Roach, Ron Riekenberg, Kevin and Nancy
MacDonald, Mike and Kathy Bloomquist, Jason Blumenthal,
Alicia R. Phillips and Sophia, Chet Pittman, Bill Kress, my
ultimate tennis doubles partner, Mark Ellgren, Troy Ephriam,
Valerie Taylor-Carter (Evans), and Doug Hennes.